Grace Anna, you, my little angel, are truly a gift from God. You have touched my heart and soul with your angelic voice of love and patriotism. I am a better man for having met you and, of course, for listening to your rendition of our national anthem. Semper fidelis!

—COL. ERNEST E. GARCIA, USMC, Ret., former Special Assistant to President Ronald Reagan

Grace Anna truly exemplifies God's grace. Her life, being, and heart-warming smile empowers us all to be beautiful, grateful, and humble in every way.

—KYRA PHILLIPS, CNN Correspondent

God has inspired me through Grace Anna's determination and strength to be what He made her to be. Her beautiful testimony and, most importantly, family made my heart smile. My love, heart, and soul are forever changed because of her silliness, gregarious laughs, and love for music. God bless Grace Anna and her family from the heavens. *Grace Anna Sings* restored me and reminded me of God's unfailing love for all of His children.

—LAUREN P. O'REILLY, The O'Reilly Foundation and O'Reilly Auto Parts

Grace Anna is the true definition of joy and strength. She always has a smile on her face no matter what battles she has had to face. She is a hero in my book.

—DIYRAL BRIGGS, Super Bowl XLV Champion

Grace Anna Sings reminds all of us that a lot of love can flow through a little heart. Grace Anna might be little, but she has a big heart and lives life in a big way! She reminds all of us that God really does put big hearts in small people and does big things in small ways. When Grace Anna sings, hearts open and heaven cheers.

—Jon Weece, Pastor,
Southland Christian Church and Author

GRACE ANNA SINGS

A story
of hope through
a little girl with
a big voice

Angela Ray Rodgers

BroadStreet
PUBLISHING

BroadStreet Publishing Group, LLC
Racine, Wisconsin, USA
BroadStreetPublishing.com

GRACE ANNʾA SINGS

Stock or custom editions of BroadStreet Publishing titles may be purchased in bulk for educational, business, ministry, fundraising, or sales promotional use. For information, please email info@broadstreetpublishing.com.

Cover photograph taken by Alex Mitro Photography (Campbellsville, KY) and used by permission. Photograph of Grace Anna with her parents and the one of Angela Rodgers on the "About the Author" page were taken by Alexa Ingram Loy Photography (Russell Springs, KY).

Cover design by Chris Garborg at garborgdesign.com
Typesetting by Katherine Lloyd at theDESKonline.com

Printed in the United States of America

17 18 19 20 21 5 4 3 2 1

*I dedicate this book to my gentle giant,
my precious peanut, and my steady rock—
the three of you are my home.*

To the advocates for people with intellectual and/or developmental disabilities who strive to give them the best life possible, you are not alone—we are in this together. To the self-advocates who face challenges most people cannot fathom, who live daily overcoming the odds—you are warriors.

CONTENTS

FOREWORD

In 2011 my husband, US Army Staff Sergeant Jamie Jarboe, was shot by a sniper on his third deployment in Afghanistan. The bullet severed his spinal cord and left him instantly paralyzed from the chest down. Months after his injury, it became my personal mission to learn everything I could to provide the quality of care my husband deserved. Unfortunately, the level of care I was able to provide wasn't enough to save his life, and he took his last breath on March 21, 2012.

Little did I know how everything I had learned would serve a greater purpose. I carried on his dying wish to help his fellow service members by caring for others with paralysis or medical conditions. I remember driving to a rural part of Kentucky to meet with Grace Anna, her mother Angela, her father Jeff, and her brother Isaiah right before Thanksgiving. As a parent, the challenges are definitely familiar to me, yet the adversity of Grace Anna's condition and the determination of her family was inspirational.

Grace Anna Sings comes as a compelling story of devotion in a vitally important time. Perhaps never before has the foundation of the family's faith been more important to the future of America.

With each passing birthday Grace Anna celebrates, I feel blessed to have been graced by their presence and know they will forever be a part of my family.

Melissa D. Jarboe
Founder, Military Veteran Project

OUR MIRACLE

Due to mistakes I made as a young woman, I spent a big chunk of my life questioning my path. I was still holding on to guilt for sins already forgiven, but I wouldn't accept God's mercy. After a failed marriage, I had given up on love and having other children. My son, Isaiah, had not.

When I met Jeff, the life I created for Isaiah and myself changed. It started out full of joy and promise; I allowed someone to love me, and I let down my guard to trust again. After three heartbreaking miscarriages, our world changed. My once-solid marriage came under tremendous strain as we tried to grieve the losses.

Then God's grace appeared.

Isaiah had been praying for a sibling since he was very young, hoping to have someone in his family beside his parents. His pure-hearted request would shortly be granted, healing hurt both Jeff and I were feeling.

Although doctors held no hope our sweet baby would make it to term, I relied upon God to carry her home to us. What I never expected was how His gift to our family would not only change our lives, but the lives of millions of people around the world.

Grace Anna came into this world, perplexing everyone even before she was born. Doctors had no idea how to explain what they saw as she grew in my tummy. They doubted she would ever take her first breath, but God had bigger plans.

Once she arrived, fighting for every breath she took, she continued to stump doctors and specialists alike. She would spend her future days doing the same, showing others miraculous things come in unexpected vessels sometimes.

We couldn't have known it at the time, but through her resilient spirit and sweet songs, this unique child would eventually change the way the world looks at those who don't fit the "normal" mold. The world would soon find out it could learn valuable lessons through a girl who defied the odds.

Our family would grow stronger, and the compassion from people around the globe would give us hope for what the world can become. Even when faced with daggers of cruel insults and attacks, love would win.

Grace Anna's talent and unbreakable happiness give hope to others where they cannot find it in today's sometimes cruel world. Her physical limitations do not stop her from experiencing life and being a light for the world.

As Grace Anna says, "It'll be okay, Momma."

Grace Anna's story has been narrowly defined by what is seen through television, the Internet, and radio, but it is only part of her story. The entire story is much more profound than just her talented singing and infectious personality.

Her story was destined to be told in its entirety. A light that shines as bright as hers cannot be hidden; it was meant for the entire world to see and witness. Her story could be the light that makes a difference for someone needing a touch of hope.

Meet our miracle, our Grace Anna, and hear her spirit sing.

FROM DESPAIR
TO JOY

The first time I met Jeff, it was like something out of a movie: sparks flew and music filled the air. I was playing volleyball at a friend's house when he pulled up in a sharp black Chevy truck with Fleetwood Mac's "The Chain" blaring from the radio. Something about him caught me completely off guard. I looked at him and then turned to my cousin. "I'm going to marry that man," I said. Of course, she laughed at me and told me I was a complete idiot. But I didn't care. I knew he was my man.

Funny thing was, I had basically sworn off men completely, having recently been through a devastating divorce. Being young and delusional, Freddie and I jumped into marriage with both feet. Unfortunately, even though I adored him, neither of us knew the first thing about marriage. And while we certainly shared times of laughter and delight, especially after our son, Isaiah, was born, a lot of tremendously dark days also plagued us. And even though I was committed to stay, Freddie wanted out.

When Freddie left, it crushed me, and I vowed that I would never again set myself up for that kind of hurt. But all that changed when I saw Jeff pull up in his truck that day. I can't explain it except to say that he felt like home.

Within six months, we started dating and the journey wasn't always easy. It was a learning process for both of us, mixed with flashes of pure joy. Jeff had never been around children much, and his initial interactions with Isaiah were quite awkward. Over time, however, he and Isaiah found things to do together, like playing ball and hunting. I knew there were moments when we both wanted to walk away, but something always pulled us back together—a feeling that life would not be the same if we were not together. Looking back now, I can't help but think God already knew Grace was on her way, and we both needed her in our lives for very distinct reasons.

Jeff and I were married on April 4, 2008, in a small celebration for family and friends. I had always hoped to have more children, but I knew going into the marriage that Jeff did not. He felt we were too old to add to our family at this stage in life. While I didn't necessarily agree, I respected his position. So you can imagine what a shock it was when, within two months of being married, Jeff asked, "When are we having a baby?"

I was dumbfounded. Was he serious? For years he had been totally against having children, but now all the sudden he wanted a baby? I was thirty-five-years old, and Isaiah was almost a teenager. Not to mention, my body wasn't what it used to be! But as I thought about it, I realized that as an only child and only grandchild on both sides of his family, Jeff would love for a child to carry on the family name and add to his very small family circle.

After weeks of prayer, I told Jeff I was ready to try to have a baby. I didn't know the journey to having a baby would be an uphill struggle.

I first became pregnant in July of 2008, and everything seemed perfect. We heard the heartbeat and even had an opportunity to see an early ultrasound. I had a few complications with bleeding but nothing that seemed serious or concerning.

When I went in for my routine three-month checkup, however, the doctor had trouble finding the heartbeat. As he moved the fetal Doppler around my abdomen, no sound emitted from it, and I knew something wasn't right. A few moments later, the nurses brought in the ultrasound machine.

As he probed my body, the doctor quietly asked, "Are you by yourself today?"

I immediately wept uncontrollably. "No, my dad is with me."

The doctor and the nurse left the room to find my dad while I got up, dressed, and sat in the stiff chair in the cold, clinical room. It was as if the air had completely disappeared from the room. I couldn't breathe, and I felt as if my lungs could not expand to fill with oxygen.

My dad entered the room, looking puzzled. "What's going on?"

"I don't know, Dad. The doctor will be back in a minute."

When Doctor Voss opened the door, I could tell the news wasn't good. He told us my unborn baby had died earlier in the week, and my fluid was slowly leaking from my body. I needed to have a D&C or try to lose the baby on my own. I believe in miracles, so at that moment I could not allow them to surgically remove my child from my body.

Dad took me into his arms as I sobbed profusely. I truly believe he felt as much sorrow at that moment as I did. We sat frozen in time, waiting for something to cue us to get up and go home. I tried to hold onto hope and not give in to the loss, but deep in my heart I knew my child was already home with Jesus.

I told the doctor that if I hadn't miscarried over the weekend, I would come back on Monday. If tests still showed the baby was deceased, I would get the D&C. It was Labor Day weekend, so I went home, propped my feet up, and waited.

The usual cookouts and family get-togethers didn't happen that year.

I didn't miscarry on my own, so the following week I was admitted to the hospital. My sweet child was taken from my body and discarded. If I had known what they do with miscarried babies, I would have requested to take his or her remains home with me for a proper burial. Amid the grief, I didn't think about what happened after they left with my baby.

The doctor called me a few weeks later and explained that a

chromosomal mutation caused the miscarriage. Evidently there was nothing we could have done to prevent it from happening. He suggested we wait at least three months to allow my body to heal, and then we could try again.

As Isaiah wept in my lap, I questioned why this was happening. I trusted that God was in control, but I was not happy with His plan at the moment. I had tried to live my life as close to Him as I could, following His Word in every area. Why would He allow this to happen to me? I had no idea God was building strength in me that would help me nurture an amazing little soul one day.

Jeff was as heartbroken as I was. He tried to be strong for me and was positive we could try again. He never let on that he struggled to accept the reality that he would never hold our baby. He believed he had to make sure Isaiah and I were okay first. This willingness to care for us was one of the reasons I fell so in love with him, but at this juncture, I also knew he needed to grieve with us. I was afraid if he didn't acknowledge how much he was hurting, the pain would consume him.

He never did acknowledge his pain.

Months passed, and we were eager to try again. It didn't take long, and we were pregnant again. We shared the news at Thanksgiving, and our families were ecstatic, especially Isaiah. He had been so wounded after the first miscarriage, the news eased his little soul. In addition, Jeff's dad's health was declining, and we prayed he would get to meet this baby.

We were relieved at our first appointment to hear that the heartbeat was strong and nothing was amiss. On Christmas Eve, we celebrated the season, and our joy at my aunt Inga's with karaoke, of course. After my rendition of "Jolene" by Dolly Parton, I made a trip to the restroom and there it was.

Blood.

I wasn't hurting, so I told myself it was just early spotting. I tried not to allow the last miscarriage to send me into a spiral of panic. But even so, I wanted to be safe, so Jeff and I headed to the emergency room. They drew my blood. The emergency room doctor couldn't find the heartbeat, but he assured us that often this early in a pregnancy, it isn't always possible to hear it. We had to wait for the lab results to know for sure what was happening.

Then I saw my cousin Sarah rounding the corner. Sarah was a lab technician at the hospital and has always had the sweetest spirit. She made eye contact with me and I knew. She was trying not to show her emotions, but as she hugged me, the tears started to flow. My HCG level was not high enough at this point in my pregnancy to indicate a viable pregnancy.

Of all the mornings to find out we had lost another baby, Christmas would now bring an unwelcome memory for the rest of our lives. I got dressed, and we started home. I cried most of the way home. Jeff never said a word, but as we eased into the driveway at 4:00 a.m., he began to wail. I had never heard such sorrow. It was a deep, mournful cry as he gasped for breath between sobs. We sat in the truck for what seemed an eternity before finally moving to the house where we went straight to bed.

I dreaded telling Isaiah, especially on Christmas, so we waited until he returned from his visit with his dad the next day. I wished I had never told him I was pregnant. His big heart had experienced more than enough hurt for an eleven-year-old, and as I explained what had happened, gigantic tears streamed down his innocent, sweet face. I held him in my arms as his body shook in disbelief. I felt as if my insides were on fire. The anger building up made me want to scream, but I knew I couldn't do that to him. He couldn't take any more pain.

Two days later, I miscarried the baby at home, and this time the grief was almost more than I could bear. I was short with people, started having panic attacks, and became very depressed. There were no support groups in our area for people who experience miscarriages, and most people didn't even bring it up. They almost acted like it was a bad word. Our family was grieving tremendously—grieving over the fact we would never hold our child or see her sweet face—and no one would acknowledge it. It was as if I had lost a tooth, not a baby.

Jeff and I were never quitters, so in spite of the pain we still experienced, it came as no surprise to our families when we were yet again pregnant in March of 2009. This pregnancy didn't even make it to eight weeks. By the time I miscarried, I was numb. I tried to focus my energies on being a top-notch teacher and a great mom to Isaiah. But none of my efforts could fill the emptiness that crept in. For some reason, I found myself angry at Jeff. My grief and ever-changing hormones made it hard to think rationally. I was finished trying to get pregnant, but he wasn't. I also worried I was being punished for mistakes I had made during my youth. I should have known better than that. God doesn't work that way.

For some reason, the shower has always been a place where I feel the freest to pray and reach out to God. As the water washes away the dirt and grime of the day, I find that it also washes away some of the pain inside. After months of these nightly shower sessions, I started to feel a little more like myself, and I realized Jeff was suffering as much as I was.

He never voiced how much pain he was in, but his sleepwalking had reached an all-time high. I often caught him walking around the room, searching under the bed, or pulling the covers off, thinking something was in the bed. He barely slept. What made things even worse was that his dad's health was declining very quickly. I knew he feared his dad would never hold a grandchild.

As the months went by, Jeff stopped talking about getting pregnant. Every once in a while, he would ask if I was ready, but I replied with an adamant no. Part of me felt selfish, but another part felt I had earned the right to say no. I had miscarried three babies in less than a year. I deserved a break.

You know that old saying about the best-laid plans? Well, my plan was not to get pregnant again. No matter what. But God, of course, had other ideas.

I stared at the pregnancy test as if it was an alien. How could this be?

We had tried to prevent this from happening. I was not prepared to lose another baby. My spirit could not handle one more miscarriage. As I continued to stare at the pink lines, I found myself becoming very angry with Jeff. I needed someone to blame, and since he was the only other person involved, he became my target.

I left the test on the counter and let him find it on his own when he came home from work. When he did, he was beyond happy—ready to celebrate. I was not. How could he think everything would be okay? Did he not know what the past year had been like? Had he forgotten the nights in the hospital—the anguish we lived through? I wished I could be happy with him, but the only thing I felt was fear.

We decided not to tell Isaiah until the second trimester this time. I couldn't live with myself if he had to endure this all over again. He had hoped for a sibling his entire life and had been let down three times already. I wasn't going to rob him of his hope.

The first two months went by without any issues. The heartbeat was strong and everything went well except for the horrible nausea and vomiting. I hadn't been sick with any of my previous pregnancies, except Isaiah's. I started to gain faith that maybe this baby would make it. I continued my daily shower prayer sessions, and as we selectively shared the news, people throughout our community and church prayed for this pregnancy. Every day, I received messages and phone calls from friends claiming that this child would make it in Jesus' name. A firestorm of optimism covered us.

While my pregnancy advanced, Jeff's dad's health worsened. He was placed in hospice, and we knew that even if our child made it, he would probably never meet her. He fought with everything he had to hold onto life until the baby arrived, but only time would tell if his body could hold out that long.

Due to my age and my history of miscarriages, my doctor sent me to see a specialist. On February 23, 2010, they ran blood work and performed a high-resolution ultrasound, and as the doctor began clicking images, I noticed he kept going back to the baby's right leg and arm. He wasn't saying much, but was taking many, many images. He excused himself from the room and returned with a nurse. I began to cry.

Jeff looked at me, "What is the matter?"

"There is something wrong with the baby," I told him. "He keeps reassessing the same thing over and over. I just know it."

Jeff was in complete denial. He tried to calm my nerves, but I knew better. I had been here before. Something wasn't right. Moments later the doctor returned and explained to us that the baby's arms and legs were not measuring what they should be for this stage of the pregnancy. He also noticed some abnormalities with the shape of the spine, feet, and head. It was all a very clinical account of what the ultrasound showed. He could tell us the baby was a girl, which made me cry even more. A sweet girl—my sweet girl resting in my belly—needed a touch from God.

The doctor went on to talk about our options, including abortion. We both firmly said no. It didn't matter what the ultrasound showed; that was our baby girl. We would pray and believe God would bring her through this. We lost three of our dear babies. This was a new chance. We would not throw our girl to the side, just because she didn't fit a doctor's idea of "normal."

Later that night, we told Isaiah the entire story. We wanted him to be prepared and understand that if I carried her full term, she may be different than what people expected, but that wouldn't change the fact that she was his sister. The joy that beamed from his soul lit up the room.

"Mom, this baby is going to make it. I know it," he said. He always had the most amazing faith for a young child.

We phoned our friends and family who had been praying, and they agreed to continue to pray for God's touch on the baby. For the first time since Jeff and I were married, I felt an amazing sense of peace and calm envelop us. I looked at my husband, and I saw a hero, a man who stood by my side through it all—the good and the bad. I realized that for far too long, my grief had clouded my view of just how wonderful he was.

Finally, we drove over to see Jeff's parents, Wyatt and Norma Jean. Wyatt was in a hospital bed in the living room, hanging on to life. We told him he was going to have a granddaughter, and his beautiful face broke out into the biggest smile you can imagine.

Five days later, Wyatt Rodgers took his last breath and went to be with Jesus. I like to think that as his spirit left his body, he got a glimpse of our precious baby girl somehow. I knew more than anyone that life was given and life was taken away, but sometimes it felt so unfair.

We had been through two very long years of marriage full of sorrow and despair, but little did we know that very soon, all that heartache would be healed. God was leading us to a special child who would not only change our lives but the lives of millions of people around the world.

2

NOT YOUR USUAL GAL

After the heartbreaking loss of Jeff's dad, our family was not yet finished with difficult times or tough decisions. I spent many days listening to the hopelessness most of our doctors seemed to focus on. Few gave us any glimmer of optimism that our unborn child would make it into this world, much less take a breath after she was born.

Besides my OB-GYN, I saw specialists to help with the delivery. One doctor reminded us every visit that we had options. We continually told the doctor we were not interested in abortion, but he still would not let it go. After one late-afternoon visit, I had heard enough. I marched to the front desk and told them, "Find me another doctor."

From then on, a new specialist handled my pregnancy. I made it clear to him during the first visit that I did not want to hear about abortion, amniocentesis, or anything else that wasn't about helping us have a safe delivery. He was more than gracious. I found myself looking forward to our conversations when we went for visits. He was very informative and supportive throughout the remainder of the pregnancy.

My body was not quite as cooperative as my new specialist. I spent every day sick from the time my feet hit the floor in the morning until I closed my eyes at night. My OB-GYN even prescribed medicine to help me keep food down. It did not help. The headaches were excruciating. My heart raced, and most days the rate was at 130 to 160 bpm. Some days I honestly did not know if my body could take much more.

At six months, following my second hospital stay to get fluids and treat my racing heart, my OB-GYN took me off work and put me on complete bed rest. I don't think people truly understood how difficult those days were for me. I had always prided myself on being a strong, independent woman. Many assumed I was fine. I wasn't. I missed teaching and interacting with people. I missed going to church, gardening, and doing as I pleased. As I lay there alone, I became fearful of what the future would hold for my child and our family. Doubts flooded my mind.

What if I can't take care of a baby with health problems? I'm not equipped for that.

What if I should leave my job, and we lose our home?

Isaiah needs me. I'm missing all his baseball games and school events. What kind of mother does that?

I found myself spending more time worrying than focusing on taking care of my health. I couldn't eat or sleep, and my heart pounded so hard I was sure I would never make it to see our sweet girl's face. My emotions were getting the best of me, and somehow, I had forgotten all about prayer.

The longer I lay there, the tougher it seemed to find peace or joy and easier to dive into self-pity.

God, where are you? Why is this happening to me? Haven't I been a good servant?

I was on the edge of spiraling down into depression. I recognized the signs and knew I had to do something to stop the pattern of my thoughts and behaviors.

I began to pray more and speak positively. When an upsetting thought crossed my mind, I refused to give into it. I would call friends or family members and ask about their day. I tried to focus on others instead of only me. Plenty of other people facing very tough struggles could use a friendly voice and welcoming ear.

I noticed a change in my attitude and how I felt. My family noticed it too. I was laughing again, smiling again, eating better, and sleeping. Life was not as horrible as my racing mind had convinced me. I started to believe everything would be okay.

We were coming upon our last scheduled ultrasound before the baby's due date. This was the ultrasound that the doctor felt would be the final indicator of whether our child could survive outside my womb. They would be looking for her lung-to-heart ratio. The previous night I stood in my shower, crying out to God to touch my unborn baby—to help her lungs and heart be the right size to make it in this world. As the hot water cleansed my body, it also seemed it washed away any doubt that tomorrow would bring good news.

God, please, I won't complain. I'll be the best mom I can possibly be. Give me a chance to be a mom again, one more time. I sobbed.

The next day we arrived at the doctor's office, and the doctor began the ultrasound. As he clicked through different images of her, he seemed very positive. Sure enough, our little fighter had a ratio that he felt would sustain life once she was born, but he was very adamant about having a C-section. Her vertebrae could be damaged with a regular birth and cause her neck to break.

"Of course, I'll have a C-section. Whatever it takes. I'm just so glad for this news."

Tears streamed down my cheeks. I knew I would see my sweet daughter. It didn't matter to me how she got there. I was overjoyed that she soon would be here. Jeff was visibly shaken. He's not one to shed many tears, but that day they were flowing. We finally were going to have a baby.

"Hallelujah, hallelujah!" I cried as I shook my hands into the air. Joy overcame my body. My enthusiasm overflowed, and the poor doctor was caught in my hugging frenzy.

The celebration lasted a few moments, then we had to plan. It relieved me some to hear I would have a C-section. I had one when Isaiah was born, so I knew what to expect.

We also had to get our home baby-ready. We immediately filled it with every newborn item we could find. My sister, Bobbie, hosted a shower for us. We were all prepared for the arrival of our sweet girl. Now it was a waiting game until the first week of August. I was due to deliver August 7.

I had to be careful of how much excitement I allowed myself to experience due to still being on bed rest. Every now and then I would sneak a trip to her new room and just marvel at how Jeff and Isaiah had pulled the room together for our sweet girl while I was keeping myself and our baby safe.

The night of July 18, 2010, a strong storm blew through and caused quite a bit of damage—enough that it knocked out our electricity. I spent the night on our couch with all the windows open and my leg hanging out one of them. The air and rain from the outside would blow in at times, relieving me from the heat and humidity. Jeff was at the end of our couch, sitting up watching over me. It was a comical sight to see.

The electricity finally came on around 4:00 a.m. I stayed on the couch as Jeff closed the windows and went back to our bed. I awoke to Isaiah rubbing my forehead around 10:00 a.m. "Mom, are you okay?"

"Yes," I told him, "I just feel a little ragged. Why do you ask?"

"You look really tired, Mom, and it's after ten o'clock. You are usually awake by seven."

I needed to get up to go to the restroom and when I did, it happened. My water broke. Just one problem. No car. My car was in the shop being fixed, Jeff was at work, and my mother-in-law, Norma Jean, was nowhere to be found. I called Jeff frantically, "Honey, come home now! She's on her way!"

"Are you sure?"

"My water broke, and I'm having pretty severe labor pains."

I don't remember him saying anything else. I heard a dial tone. Within ten minutes Jeff was at the house, and we were on our way to the local hospital. We feared if we tried to make it to our scheduled hospital in Lexington, she would be born on the way. The possibility of a natural child birth was not ideal, so we thought we should go to a local hospital to be on the safe side.

"What if she's already on her way? I must have a C-section. She can't survive a regular birth," I sobbed to Jeff.

Jeff tried his best to calm me down. "She's going to be all right. Hang in there."

I didn't know anything else to do except pray and get my family and friends to do the same.

Once we arrived at Somerset, the doctors felt we could make it to Lexington. Part of me was terrified to get back on the road and attempt to make it to Lexington in time for her to be delivered. Jeff wasn't that worried. He stopped by a McDonald's on the way to get a Big Mac, which irritated me to no end.

"What are you doing?"

"I'm hungry."

"Well, if this baby comes out of me before we get to Lexington, it's not going to be pretty for you."

He was as cool as a cucumber, and I was frantic. The labor pains were getting closer and more painful, and my husband was absolutely getting on my last nerve.

My regular OB-GYN was on vacation in Colorado, so we had to see a doctor I had never met before. He immediately sent me to the hospital to be checked in.

There must have been a full moon that day, because the nurses informed us they were absolutely bursting at the seams with babies being born. We checked in to a holding room where doctors and nurses monitored the baby and me.

My dad and his wife, my sister, my niece, my nephew, Isaiah, Jeff, and me packed the room. Oh, it was loud. The tougher the labor pains got, the louder my family seemed to get. Jeff would rub my back, but somehow it made it worse. I was trying to be nice, but I wanted to scream. Everybody was happy and laughing, having a good time, and I felt as if a knife were being stabbed in my lower back. Not to mention, I was concerned that something would go amiss.

All I wanted to do was hold my precious baby and kiss her sweet face. God had blessed me with the opportunity to be a mom again, and I could not wait to see the beautiful soul He had planned for me to nurture. This little girl would be an answered prayer not just for me but for our entire family. The amount of healing her life would provide was heavy on my heart. Losing four babies had left a hole in my heart that this little girl would most definitely fill.

I noticed the baby's heart rate was getting high and that the nurses were coming in more frequently. My heart rate also started to skyrocket. The last time a nurse came in, she seemed concerned. "We're going to get you in a room right now. You can't wait any longer."

I was wheeled into an operating room and given something to relax me, which did not seem to do its job. I felt no different than before they gave it to me. After three attempts, the anesthesiologist finally got my saddle block in and the caesarean section began.

The doctor moved quickly to pull our daughter from my body. I found it odd they never showed me her face. I knew with our medical history she would go straight to the NICU, but I figured they would at least show me her face first.

"Mrs. Rodgers, the other doctors took your daughter to be examined in another room. We will go ahead with the tubal ligation. Are you feeling okay?" the doctor asked.

"Yes, I'm okay. When can I see my daughter?"

"When we get you through this and back in a room, we will see about getting your daughter to you."

They moved through the procedure calmly and walked me through each step. The room was very cold, and I was nauseous from the anesthesia. I kept wondering how our baby was doing, and I was ready for them to be finished and get me to my room. I drifted in and out of consciousness as the procedure continued. Machines beeping and the sound of surgical equipment distracted my mind for moments, but I was still focused on getting to my child.

The next thing I remember was waking up in my room with my

legs still a little numb. I tried to kick and move them around. The quicker I was back to myself, the quicker I could go see my girl.

"Wake up, legs!" I screamed, "my daughter needs me."

Jeff sat at my bedside, holding my hand and smiling. I was perplexed. I knew I couldn't hold her, because I wasn't fully back to myself yet, but why was he sitting there? Why wasn't he with our daughter? I knew him. He was as excited as I was to see her, so it made no sense why he was still by my side. None of my family was coming in either. What was going on?

Then a knock on the door came. "Mr. Rodgers, can I see you a moment?" a doctor asked.

"I'll be back in a minute, honey," he told me as he left the room. Jeff returned with tears rolling down his cheeks. I suddenly became very frightened at what was happening.

"What's wrong?" I yelled. "Where is she?"

He smiled. "She's okay, but we have to go see her."

I had no idea that since they pulled our daughter from my belly, she had been fighting to survive. She had swallowed meconium (the baby's first stool from the waste in the uterus) during delivery. Doctors had pulled her into the NICU to save her life the moment she was born. She had been fighting for her life the entire time, and I didn't know it. My husband did know, however. He had known the entire time. He had been protecting me and didn't want me to know anything until they were sure what was going to happen.

"It's going to be okay, honey; our girl is here," he cried.

I sobbed uncontrollably. I wanted to see her right then. I didn't want to wait anymore. I ached to feel her body against mine and to see her sweet face. I wanted to hear her cry and smell her breath. My soul yearned to bond with my daughter, and I was not going to take no for an answer.

Jeff left the room to find the doctors and returned with a pediatrician who told us we could go see her in a few moments, but first he felt he needed to prepare us for what we were getting ready to see.

"I've never seen a child born with some of things your daughter has," he explained. "She has scales on most of her body and has some physical abnormalities."

"What do you mean?" I asked.

"Your daughter has something, and I have no idea what it is. She is breathing on her own and is stable, but I don't know what we are dealing with. I want you to be prepared to see her."

The doctor was not trying to be hurtful; he was just trying to make sure we were informed of everything going on with her.

It didn't matter to me what she looked like. I would love her any way she came. My soul ached to be in the room with her. She was special no matter what the doctor or anyone else thought.

The nurses helped me into a wheelchair and pushed me down the hallway to the NICU, full of newborn babies with struggles of their own. Then I saw my girl. My body trembled when I finally saw the angel for whom I had prayed so many times. My heart's desire was snuggled in a blanket with wires and monitors all over her.

The nurses helped place her into my arms, and life as I had known it completely changed. My little girl would not be your usual little girl; she would be unique. She was going to face things that would not be easy, but that didn't bother me. I wasn't just holding a newborn, I was holding a warrior.

A peace like I had never known filled my body. It was as if she and I were the only two people in the room. She never cried. She lay there peaceful and calm, holding my finger tightly in her hand. It was as if she knew she would be just fine and there was no need for us to be anxious. God had this.

I studied her face and body, wondering why the doctor was so concerned. Some yellow scales did appear on her fingers. The skin was pulled so tightly it looked as if she had six fingers instead of five. Her sweet nose seemed so tiny, and her bright eyes were swollen from the delivery. She hovered a little on the short side—a whopping fifteen and a half inches long—but she was pudgy at six pounds and five ounces. She held her right arm in like a little bird with an injured wing. I could tell she was protecting it.

Maybe I gazed at her through eyes of a momma's love, and the doctor evaluated her through clinical eyes. I saw the issues, but I also saw her spirit. She was a fighter, and I knew God had sent her to me, chosen me to be her momma. She would make a difference in this world. Those little physical abnormalities did not discourage my faith in God. I trusted He would use her in a mighty way.

Isaiah came into the room a few moments later. It is no accident he was chosen to be her brother. Isaiah prayed for her from the moment he knew I was pregnant. His precious thirteen-year-old spirit soared to see his baby sister.

"I told you, Mom." He placed his hand across her cheek. "I've known all along my sister would be fine." His remarkable faith and love made me proud to be his momma. I could never ask for a better son, and my daughter had gained a lifelong protector in him.

The next morning the pediatrician came to our room and informed us he was transferring her to the University of Kentucky (UK) NICU. He told us, "I have no idea what your daughter has, and I feel they can help her more than we can here."

They rolled me into the room to see her before she was loaded into the ambulance. It broke my heart to see her taken away. Having that itty-bitty girl ride in the ambulance without one of us seemed brutal to me. I know it was what she needed, but I wanted to hop up and go with her.

The nurses at UK were incredible. Our girl thrived under their care. She was alert, drinking well, and voiding properly. An ultrasound of her internal organs showed they were functioning normally. Scales covered her body except for her beautiful face and plump bottom. It turns out the skin disorder ichthyosis was so severe on her right hand that it had pulled one finger to a bent position. It's very aggressive and builds up layers of rough skin that will not fall off without a regimen of skin emollients. She would deal with this her entire life.

Then the doctors shared more bad news. "We feel there is a possibility your daughter is blind. We cannot find a reflection from her retinas. This usually means they have not developed correctly. We must do further testing to find out what exactly is going on."

After five days in the NICU, our daughter was thriving. The only problem was doctors still couldn't figure out her condition or why she couldn't see. Until they found out what was going on with her, she couldn't go home. We wanted to get home desperately, but we also wanted to know what was going on with our daughter.

On the sixth day, a geneticist interviewed us and examined her. Within an hour of the interview and examination, she knew what it was. Chondrodysplasia punctata. Yes, that's a mouthful, and few people have ever heard of it.

Chondrodysplasia punctata is a group of disorders characterized by the formation of small hardened spots of calcium on the inside of the cartilage or on the heads of long bones. Varying reasons can cause the different forms of the disorder.

All her signs and symptoms were identifiers for the genetic disorder, even the lack of reflection from the retinas. She wasn't blind; she had cataracts. She had the possibility of seeing, but it would require surgery within a few months. Along with the cataracts, she had a flattened nasal bridge, stippling in her bones, shortened limbs, shortened fingers, shortened toes, ichthyosis, sparse hair, and misshapen bones. It was quite a lot to take in.

The geneticist explained that she knew of three forms of the disorder, and without testing, we would not be able to identify which type it was. They would have to do a biopsy of a small section of her skin. We struggled over the decision to allow this. She assured us it would cause minimal pain for her, so we agreed to the testing.

"I feel she more than likely has the recessive form of the disorder," the geneticist told us. "Her legs are the same length. Most of the time this appears in the recessive form. If this is the type, your daughter will have a short life span, not more than ten years."

I was in shock. What was that doctor thinking? Could she not see how great she was doing? I refused to accept the outcome. Jeff and I decided not to tell Isaiah the prognosis until we knew. He had been through enough, and I was not about to upset him when I wholeheartedly believed she would prove them wrong.

At first Jeff struggled to believe she would be fine. He had moments of despair at night. Not only was he dealing with the possibility of his daughter living only a few years, he was still trying to grieve his dad's passing. He had dramatic episodes of sleepwalking where I would talk him back into bed. His heart was so heavy. I had to be strong for both of us.

Our extended family was committed to pray with us for God to move. We prayed the results would prove she had another form of the disorder in which she could live a long and happy life.

Each day I prayed for God to touch our daughter and help us through this. I sang to her any moment fear crept in. I would praise God through the rain. My baby would not have the recessive form. I would not accept it. People in our church and community prayed for us, called us, checked on us, and sent prayer cloths.

The weeks progressed, and she grew steadily, sleeping most days and drinking like a little piglet. She showed no signs of being a weak baby. The little bundle of joy confirmed my belief that she would be fine. God had this.

Then the phone rang.

The geneticist was puzzled. She did have a form of chondrodysplasia punctata, but it wasn't the recessive form. It was the dominant form, Conradi-Hünermann. The doctor could not believe the results because of her legs and arms.

Conradi-Hünermann syndrome keeps the body from breaking down cholesterol correctly. This had caused the medical problems she was having. She would deal with medical issues, and more than likely surgeries, but with the right medical help, she could live a very long life.

My mom and a friend sat in the living room with me. I hung up the phone and began jumping and praising God. He had been in control the entire time. He knew what would happen with our daughter. We all embraced each other, praising the Lord together.

I called Jeff and told him the amazing news, and like me, he wept. I sat Isaiah down and explained what had been going on. Once again, the faith of a child is much stronger at times than for us adults.

"Mom, I told you she would be fine. Why didn't you believe me?"

"Because we are stinking old adults, I guess." I gave him a smile and a hug. I was reminded by his loving, trusting heart that I would have to let go of the worry and start fully relying on God to take care of my daughter and my family.

Although her diagnosis may not have seemed a blessing to some, it blessed us. In our minds, she was a miracle. We had waited a long time for this precious child, and we determined to make her life as full as we possibly could. Just because she didn't fit society's norm didn't mean she couldn't have an abundant life full of joy and hope.

The mountains to climb came very quickly. She had cataracts on both eyes. We began to research Conradi-Hünermann, but we couldn't find much. We could never have imagined that we would become educators to doctors instead of doctors teaching us about her disorder. Finding doctors who had even heard of Conradi-Hünermann syndrome was a rarity. I don't know why it surprised us. We were now faced with choosing doctors that would not only treat our daughter but want the best life for her. What we found were doctors that were much like our daughter, exceptional and extraordinary.

Our lives had taken a whirlwind of a ride, but God delivered us through it all. This life experience is how we named our daughter. Jeff had never met his grandmother Anna due to her death early in life, so Anna was chosen to be part of her name. Then came her first name. We had been through so much in our few years together, we felt we had survived it by the grace of God. So, there it was, her name: Grace. God had given us a gift of love. Little did we know she would touch people across the world and heal hurts that had existed for many years. She was our miracle, our answered prayer, our Grace Anna.

3

TOUGH CHOICES

We had made it through the first two months with Grace Anna without any major hiccups. Grace Anna grew wonderfully, doing what most newborns do: eating, sleeping, pooing, and peeing. I enjoyed every moment. I knew the upcoming months could possibly bring rough times, so I gobbled up the quiet days.

During those quiet days when Grace Anna napped, I would search the Internet for anything I could find about Conradi-Hünermann syndrome. It was frightening. It seemed no two sites could agree on much of anything. I soon realized I was getting myself worked up over nothing. We needed to find someone with the disorder, locate good doctors, and be diligent to gather accurate information.

Our first challenge was to find a pediatrician with experience with Conradi-Hünermann syndrome. I learned very quickly that unless we wanted to travel three to four hours a day for a pediatrician, we needed to find a local doctor willing to learn about the condition and wanting to provide the best care.

I questioned several friends with newborns, searching for the best pediatrician in the area. One name kept coming up, Cherice Patterson.

It's funny how we sometimes get an image in our head of what someone will look like based on their profession. I had met many doctors over the last few years, and Dr. Patterson did not fit the mold. Warm, inviting, and brilliant, we were delighted to have someone like her be Grace Anna's doctor. After our initial visit, she set up an appointment at a state hospital for an ophthalmology consult. Because of how the eyes develop, the longer we waited for surgery, the greater the possibility she would lose her vision.

We traveled to the state hospital and entered the waiting room. What struck me first was the number of adults in the waiting room. There were hardly any children. I began to get a little nervous. *Surely the children and adults do not go to the same surgeons*, I thought.

They did.

Soon we were called back. The doctor walked into the room, never identified who she was or what she was doing. She had the worst bedside manner of any doctor I've ever met.

She was not gentle with Grace Anna, and she informed me that Grace Anna would be her first cataract removal for an infant. It felt as if someone had poured hot ash all over me. I'm sure the look on my face was not a look of acceptance. "Why are you doing that?" I asked. "Is there something specific you are looking for? You've never done this before?" Then she did it. She stirred up a fire in me. She called my daughter a burden.

"Excuse me," I said. "What did you call her?"

"Well, this process is not going to be easy. You will have to get up night and day and administer eye drops. It is going to be quite difficult. It will be a burden on your family. Are you sure you want to put your family through this?"

I don't know if it was my mouth hanging wide open or my bulging eyes staring a hole through her head, but she knew I was angry.

"What is wrong with you?" I asked. "This is my daughter. I will do whatever it takes to give her the ability to see. I don't care what you say or what you think you can do, you will never touch my daughter."

I got up, tears running down my face, and left the building. One of the nurses tried to get me to come back in, but I was finished. There had to be someone better out there to take care of our girl. This doctor sure wasn't going to be one of them.

I drove home and explained to Jeff what had happened.

"What now?" he said.

"I'll call Dr. Patterson."

After speaking with me, Dr. Patterson agreed that we needed to go somewhere else. "Let me do some research, and I'll call you back tomorrow with a plan and a doctor."

As I cradled Grace Anna's tiny body against my chest, it hurt my heart to know she couldn't see any light, any shape—anything at all. Tears flowed down my cheeks. I didn't know what to do. I couldn't let my daughter be the first patient she performed this surgery on. I couldn't let someone with that type of callousness take care of my girl.

Lord, guide my direction and path. Help me decide for my daughter, I prayed. *Send us to the right doctors to take care of her eyes. I cannot do this without you.*

The next morning, I received an email from a friend who was taking her child to Cincinnati Children's Hospital. He also had a rare condition, and they had been very successful with treatment there. I trusted her opinion, so I called Dr. Patterson. Wouldn't you know it, she already had made Grace Anna an appointment with a doctor at Cincinnati Children's Hospital. Grace Anna was worked into the schedule very quickly due to the urgency of the eye surgery needed.

Three days later, Jeff, Grace Anna, and I sat in the patient room, nervously awaiting another discussion with another doctor. Grace Anna was snuggled up in my arms as if she had not a care in the world. She had no idea how important this day was to her future, but Jeff and I very much knew this doctor could greatly influence her quality of life.

As I sat waiting, I whispered, "Lord, send us the right doctor. Send us the one who can help Grace Anna."

After we heard a knock on the door, a tall, slender gentleman walked into the room, shook our hands, and introduced himself. "Hello, I'm Dr. Motley."

Dr. Motley's mannerisms as well as his unique glasses sure did remind me of someone. Then it hit me—Clark Kent of *Superman*. I sure was hoping he would be our superhero and tell us everything would be okay.

Dr. Motley made direct eye contact with us and was very inviting. He asked specific questions about Grace Anna and gave us time to voice our concerns and ask our questions. Remarkably, whereas the other doctor had never performed a cataract removal surgery, this one did one to two a month. It astonished me that these two cities, not extremely far apart, offered such different experience and expertise.

"Our main concern is that our daughter will be able to see," I stated.

"I see no reason she would not be able to see once she has recovered from surgery and she is fitted with corrective lenses."

Dr. Motley probably thought we were half crazy, because once he expressed confidence that Grace Anna would be able to see, I became ecstatic—crying, clapping, laughing. All my emotions were supercharged with joy. It was a sight to see. His slight chuckle of delight at my reaction opened a door of comfort with a doctor that I've never quite experienced.

There was no mention of her being a burden or the process being extremely difficult. He explained there would be eye drops and some risks of glaucoma, but these things could be addressed. It was so encouraging to know he would be taking care of our girl.

The next week was surgery time.

We went through all the forms and discussions of risks of surgery, benefits of surgery, and postsurgery instructions. The staff at Cincinnati Children's Hospital was extremely detailed and prepared parents very well. Grace Anna's first surgery would require an overnight stay, because she was so young and due to her unknown reactions to sedation.

As I dressed her in her little gown for presurgery, I kissed her sweet face many times. At Cincinnati, parents could walk their child to the surgery room and be with them as they went under sedation, so I slipped on my gown and mask as did Jeff. We were all ready to do this together.

Lord, bless the doctors and nurses through a successful surgery. Give them steady hands and wisdom, I prayed.

As the nurse walked us to the surgery room, I held Grace Anna in a tight embrace to my chest. Although I trusted the doctors, my insides felt as if they had turned to Jell-O. Still, I held fast to presenting myself as calm and collected. Grace Anna needed to feel safe and secure going into this new place, out of my arms and into the care of total strangers.

As we walked into the sterile atmosphere of the surgical room, it was very cold, very bright, and not the most inviting of places. Machines lined the walls, and a huge bed waited for my sweet little gal. It looked incredibly huge for such a tiny baby.

"We're going to take good care of her," one of the nurses said.

"Thank you. She is our little miracle," I replied. "Please let us know as soon as it's over."

"We will, and we'll also update you all through the process."

I laid Grace Anna on the bed, kissed her cheek, and told her, "I love you." The anesthesiologist placed the mask on her mouth and nose, then she drifted into a heavy sleep. My heart tightened as I watched her body relax. It didn't appear to be a sweet slumber; her fragile body seemed to collapse into a total retreat.

I pushed my way through the waiting room door and wept uncontrollably. Jeff pulled me in to hold me. A nurse rubbed my back and assured me she was in the best of hands possible. The nurse guided us to the waiting room and explained how the updates would come and where the doctor would meet us once the procedure was over.

The wait began.

Both Jeff and I checked the board many times. I tried to occupy my mind by reading some magazines and looking through my phone. It didn't help. I needed to hear a calming voice. I needed to talk to my son.

I stepped into the hall and called the school where I taught.

Isaiah was a student there now. I called the front office and asked my dear friends to get him to call his momma. Within a few moments, I heard his precious voice.

"Momma, is she okay? Can she see? Is she hurting?"

I realized he needed me to ease his mind more than I needed to be comforted.

"She's doing wonderful."

What kind of mom was I? My thirteen-year-old son was in full panic mode and had been all day. I had not even thought of how he was handling all of this.

"Are you okay?" I asked.

I could hear him sniffling and trying not to cry. "I'm okay, Mom. I just miss you all."

"As soon as she is out of recovery, I will call the school, and they will tell you. It's going to be okay. She's tough, and you've been praying, haven't you?"

"Yes, Mom."

"Then it will all be fine. Now go back to class and do your schoolwork. I'll be home as soon as I can."

I felt like a failure as a mother. I hadn't even noticed that he was overwhelmed by the whole experience. He had always been the type of child who never complained, never caused me an ounce of worry, and had been a joy to raise, but I wasn't there for him. He was my child too, and I needed to start remembering that.

As soon as I hung up the phone, the announcer said, "Grace Rodgers' family." Grace was out of surgery.

We were directed to a room where Dr. Motley waited. "She did very well. We removed the cataract. Everything went wonderfully."

"Great," Jeff said. "What happens next?"

"She will be transferred to a room and stay the night. The nurses will escort you up there when we are finished in here."

Within moments we were escorted to a private patient room. There she was. Her eye was bandaged up, and an IV came out of her tiny little wrist. She rested peacefully, so I gently rubbed her back.

Then I picked up my cell phone to call my school.

Our school secretary, Debbie, answered. "How is she doing?"

"She did really well," I said. "We have to stay the night. Please let Isaiah know she's okay, and our family friend Mark will pick him up after school."

"Absolutely."

Mark had been so amazing to our family. He took Isaiah to school for us in the mornings and picked him up in the afternoons, so I could care for Grace. Jeff's work schedule prevented him from doing it. Mark volunteered each week and would not take no for an answer. He was more like family than merely a family friend.

The room was well equipped for two parents to stay. A roll-out love seat that converted to a full bed would be Jeff's resting spot while I would occupy a rocking chair near Grace Anna's bed. I tried to rest my eyes while she did, but I just couldn't. I silently watched her sleep while I laid my head by her in the bed.

My cell phone rang around eight that evening. It was Isaiah.

"Mom, why haven't you called me?"

"We've been trying to get settled in and adapted to the room."

"Next time, call me. I've been worried. Is she doing all right?"

"Yes, Son. She is going to be fine. We will probably be home tomorrow. You're going to stay with your friend tonight. We will pick you up tomorrow."

Isaiah has always been protective of me, but when Grace Anna came along, it was different. He absolutely adored her. The first few months were very difficult for his young soul. He wanted to help so much. He just didn't know how to do it. I realized he was being treated like an adult, but he wasn't an adult. I needed to make sure he still got to be a kid. I knew when we got home, some things had to change.

It was a difficult night after the bandages came off. Eye drops were administered throughout the night, and she fought the IV in her arm. As soon as she was ready, I placed her in my arms and rocked her in the rocking chair beside her bed.

She rooted her little head into my chest and cried a soft whimper. I felt so helpless in those moments. All I could think of was to sing, so I began singing "You Are My Sunshine" softly into her ear. Slowly she stopped crying and drifted off to sleep. We finished the night with her sleeping in my arms. I only got two to three hours sleep that night. I wasn't worried about taking care of myself. She was the priority now.

Once the sunlight shone through the hospital window, we were all ready to go home. The hospital was wonderful as far as hospitals go, but we were ready to get home and sleep in our own beds. By noon, the doctors had released Grace Anna to go home. They had trained us how to administer the eye drops while at home and given us detailed postoperative instructions, which made me feel more at ease. At first I was terrified I would not be able to administer the eye drops correctly, but the nurses were stellar teachers.

We loaded up and started our three-hour trip back home. We stopped halfway to feed Grace Anna, check her eye, and change her diaper. She was very content in the car seat. I thought after surgery she might be in a grumpy mood, but she was very much the little sweetheart she had been since birth.

After a month, we returned to Cincinnati for removal of the second cataract. It went very well also. The main difference was we all got to go home that day due to Grace Anna being older and how well she did after the first surgery. Recovery for both surgeries went amazingly. The eye drops were not the most fun, but it was not as hard as I thought it would be. I knew I had to do it for Grace Anna. It is amazing sometimes what parents can overcome to help their children. I was determined to be the best mom I could be to help her be a happy girl.

I was also determined to be the best mom I could be for Isaiah. We all sat down as a family and decided we were going to start making time to get to his stuff too. He was important to us. I started going to his games and spending time with him, just the two of us. Jeff took him fishing again and did all the things they did before

Grace Anna. Life does change once you have a child with special health issues, but it doesn't have to be only about her. Everyone in the family needs to be important. It takes some balancing and a little work to make it happen.

We continued to go to Cincinnati Children's for treatment on Grace Anna's eyes. We even tried contacts to help her vision. It started out wonderfully, but once she got big enough to fight them, the contacts were not happening. We instead got her some cute frames to accentuate her adorable little face.

Unfortunately, within eight months of the last eye surgery, she developed glaucoma in her left eye and the cataract grew back in her right eye. There is always a chance of these things happening in children after cataract removal surgery. A new surgeon, Dr. Yang, handled the glaucoma surgery, and it went very well. Dr. Motley completed the third cataract removal. Grace Anna has not had any problems from the surgeries since the glaucoma surgery. We make biannual trips for exams and glasses. Each time, we are very impressed and grateful that God sent these doctors to us.

Even though we love Cincinnati Children's, we chose a geneticist and orthopedic surgeon closer to home. We eventually stopped seeing the geneticist, because it seemed the disorder was being studied and Grace Anna wasn't being treated. The doctor really didn't do anything to hurt Grace Anna, but she didn't do anything to help her either. To me, if a doctor isn't improving her quality of life, she doesn't need to see that provider.

We chose Shriner's Hospital in Lexington to treat Grace Anna's spine issues. My grandpa had been a Shriner, and the hospital had a strong reputation for good care. Dr. Patterson recommended Dr. Talwalkar. He was respected for being very knowledgeable and giving his patients great care. I trusted Dr. Patterson's opinion, so we decided to meet with him.

The first time I met Dr. Talwalkar, my sister, Bobbie Jo, went along with me. She is a physical therapy assistant and had been trained to help people with spine issues. I knew she would know what he was talking about and could help me ask questions to help Grace Anna's care.

When Dr. Talwalkar entered the room, he greeted us with a big smile and handshake. He immediately spoke to Grace Anna in a softer, sweeter tone. It was evident he related to his patients very well. I felt comfortable expressing my concerns and questions with him. My sister also grilled him with every question she could think of about Grace Anna's condition. It was funny watching her rattle on while Dr. Talwalkar answered each question thoroughly.

"Grace Anna is unique. There are few girls like her," he explained. "This will be a process of seeing how she grows and how her spine forms through the growing process."

"We are most concerned with handling her in a safe manner and making sure we do all we need to help her," I said.

Dr. Talwalkar continued to explain the X-rays and how her body would grow. "With Conradi, one side of the body grows faster than the other, so there is no way to know fully how her body will form or if it will be able to adapt without help from braces, surgery, or castings."

I left that day confident in his abilities as a physician. I knew he would do his best to give Grace Anna the best care possible.

We continued to see Dr. Talwalkar for several visits a year, and each time X-rays were done and analyzed. He always was very up-front about everything going on with Grace Anna's legs and spine. Sure enough, after a little over a year, Grace Anna had both legs cast from the hips down to her toes. Her feet were turning in and her legs were not straight.

We loved the staff at Shriner's. Each time she had something done, every person we encountered was always full of joy and loving with Grace Anna. I also had grown to greatly respect Dr. Talwalkar, and Grace Anna adored him. She thought he was a very cute doctor and his personality seemed to help them bond. She had nicknamed him "Dr. Cutie." It was adorable. She was closer to him than any other specialist she saw. I greatly valued his opinion and trusted that he always was very detailed in the findings of Grace Anna's condition.

The number one thing I loved about Dr. Talwalkar was that if he didn't know the answer, he would tell us. His character as a human being showed, and it was this character that would change our lives when he recommended a new orthopedic doctor for Grace Anna. It was one of the toughest decisions Jeff and I made concerning Grace Anna's health.

The first year and a half of Grace Anna's life had been very busy for our family. Sometimes I felt as if I would meet myself on the road one day going to and from doctors. Thankfully those visits brought us in contact with some of the best medical professionals on the planet.

There were moments I felt as if I had failed as a parent, but I quickly learned my children would forgive me. They still have pure hearts and don't know anything else to do but love. Each day I awoke, I prayed that God would direct my decisions as a parent and a wife. Even while going through some very tough times in our lives, we all could sit at the supper table and laugh together over something silly that had happened that day.

God had brought us through life's winding rollercoaster thus far. Little did we know, the months ahead would bring a mountain we had never climbed before.

4

ꓞIRST FLIGHT

Life sometimes has a funny way of throwing curveballs at you that seem to change the way you swing at life. Grace Anna had been doing very well, and I felt I could finally go back to teaching.

This meant I had to train someone on the ins and outs of taking care of a child with her various health issues. My mom, Kathy, and Norma Jean took turns caring for Grace Anna at first. Then my sweet cousin Ashley helped also. They all were very good with Grace Anna and did whatever I asked them to do, but I was her momma.

I felt so torn leaving her each morning. Our family needed the income I provided, but the guilt of not being there to care for her tugged at my heart daily. Sometimes during my planning hour, I would go into my storage closet and cry my eyes out. Then I would pull myself together and be the teacher my students deserved. It wasn't easy, but I knew if God wanted me at home, He would guide me in that direction.

Grace Anna was growing and developing quite well. I learned early not to compare her growth and milestones to other babies around us. She was unique and would define her own path. There is such a variance for those with Conradi-Hünermann that it is hard to compare her to other people with the genetic disorder. It barely affects some, while it affects others in the extreme. A very diverse group of people have Conradi-Hünermann.

Each day Grace Anna progressed very well, and she was soon ready for her six-month checkup with Dr. Talwalkar. I knew Grace

Anna's back was weak—we had known this from the beginning—but I had also noticed that Grace Anna didn't move her legs very much. It came as no surprise that he wanted to do a set of X-rays after we arrived. The staff at Shriner's Hospital always knew exactly how to position Grace Anna well, and they had such loving spirits. I could see these people loved what they did each day.

Once we were finished with X-rays, I carried my tiny wonder to the patient room. Then we were hit with a shocking realization. Life was getting ready to change dramatically for us once again, especially for Grace Anna.

"The X-rays reveal that Grace Anna has a vertebra shaped like a triangle pushing into her spinal cord. It is causing some of the trouble she has with her legs. Her curvature has become substantially worse also."

I searched for something to say, but I was dumbfounded. My mind raced with thoughts of my daughter paralyzed, incapable of taking care of herself, or worse, of us losing her. I could hardly get out any words at all.

"What does this mean?" I asked. "Is she going to be okay?"

"She is going to need surgery to address both issues, and I do not feel comfortable doing it myself."

Tears welled up, and I couldn't find any power within me to keep from crying. Fear overwhelmed my mind. Not my girl. She's too small. She's just a baby. I dried my eyes and looked at Jeff, who was as broken as I was. All I could do was shake my head at him. I just couldn't talk.

Jeff questioned Dr. Talwalkar. "Where do we go? Who do we take her to?"

Without hesitation Dr. Talwalkar gave us names of two doctors in the United States; neither was in Kentucky, neither was close to home. There wasn't much time to make the decision, because she needed the surgery as soon as possible.

Dr. Talwalkar tried his best to reassure us he had complete faith that both doctors would take care of Grace Anna. I respected him for admitting he was not comfortable doing the surgery. It showed he wanted the best care for Grace Anna.

He gave us some papers with information about each doctor. "Take a few days to research the doctors and let me know your decision. I'll get everything started and help the best I can."

We shook his hand, and he patted our backs. He kissed Grace Anna's forehead. "It is going to be okay."

At that moment, I could hardly find the strength to walk to our car. I kept looking at her innocent face, knowing what she was getting ready to endure. A back surgery was tough on anyone, but to put that amount of trauma on such a small, fragile child was more than I thought she should have to go through.

Once in the car, I called my sister, Bobbie. She'd been my closest confidant most of my life. She had recently faced a battle with breast cancer, and our bond as sisters had greatly grown through our hardships over the years.

"Bobbie," I sobbed. "It's her back."

"What? *What?*"

After I explained what was going on, I heard her weeping. Both she and Grace Anna had been beaten down by health issues. It created a special bond between them. My sister changed when Grace Anna came along. Going through their struggles together gave her strength to face each surgery and procedure.

"It's going to be okay, Sis. She's a fighter," Bobbie said through tears.

Within moments of talking with her, I could feel my nerves calming and my attitude changing. This surgery would help my daughter move her legs and become an independent woman one day. I would educate myself on the doctors and trust that God would take care of her. We ended our conversation, and I prayed for God's guidance.

Once we arrived home, the research began on the two doctors. Both doctors had excellent backgrounds and both were very far away from home. Either choice would be quite a haul for our family, and financially it would be very tough.

One thing kept pulling us to one doctor, though. He had a great amount of experience with people with dwarfism. If anyone knew the struggles Grace Anna faced, he would. After four days of calling specialists, reading articles online, and watching videos of the doctors, we chose the doctor we felt would best understand Grace Anna's condition.

The doctor was very experienced in orthopedic surgery and was ranked in the top ten surgeons in his specialty at the time. Once we spoke with his assistant, we had to travel to Cincinnati Children's Hospital for an MRI and CAT scan of Grace Anna's spine. Once the results were in, we planned our first trip to the big city, a ten-hour drive if we didn't stop anywhere.

With all the hectic things going on with planning and researching, it was hard to stop and breathe at times. It was also hard to find time to do things with Isaiah, which was starting to take its toll on him. I sat down with him a few weeks before the appointment in order to let him vent.

"Are you okay, Son?"

"Mom, I'm fine. Worry about Grace Anna."

"I was thinking, when we go to Baltimore, why don't you go with us?"

He paused only a few seconds. "Yes, Mom, please. I would feel so much better if I was with you all."

Granny Jean was also beyond emotional. Not only had she lost her husband a little over a year before, but now her only grandchild was facing a major surgery. So, what did we do? All four of us loaded up with Grace Anna and headed to the hospital.

The drive was long and tiresome. Jeff was exhausted as we traveled the mountainy road. Grace handled each mile well for a child her age. We would stop to let her move around and eat every two hours or so. Between conversations about the scenery and frequent naps, we were finally getting close to our hotel.

After tossing and turning all night, I awoke early to try get us some of the buffet breakfast. When I returned, my family was still sleeping away. Grace Anna rested peacefully in her bed. Her angelic face showed no signs of pain or worry. I sat by her bed, asking the Lord to touch her that day and bless the doctor we were getting ready to meet.

"I love you, my peanut," I whispered into her ear. And I rubbed my hand across her cheek. Being near her calmed any remaining anxiety I had about the day ahead. Deep down, I knew we had made the right choice and this doctor would make her life better.

Within a couple of hours, everyone was up, showered, and ready to get to the appointment. Navigating a large city is quite different than the backroads of rural Kentucky, but as with most people from Kentucky, we adapted quite well to the new surroundings.

We entered the Outpatient Center, and I checked us in. We then headed up to the doctor's office. Once paperwork was finished and insurance cards were copied, I sat down with my family and patiently waited for them to call Grace Anna back.

Grace Anna was seen by the nurse practitioner who would be getting the appointment started. She was a very friendly and warm lady, very interested in our path that led us to the doctor. She spent the first few minutes getting Grace Anna's medical history and discussing some of the protocols at the hospital.

Then we heard a knock on the door, and the doctor entered the room.

He had a very large presence in contrast with his not-so-large size. I learned very quickly that he also had a type of humor I related to, kind of ornery.

"Grace Anna is a unique girl and will need unique care," he said.

"Do you feel confident that you can fix her spine?" Jeff asked.

"Yes, absolutely."

His self-confidence may have seemed rude to some, but it reassured me we had made the right decision. I didn't want someone who doubted his abilities cutting on my daughter's back.

We met with him for around thirty minutes, discussing all aspects of the surgery and recovery. Grace Anna's lower spine would need a spinal fusion surgery. A fusion is where a bridge is made between two or more vertebrae next to each other. After an examination of Grace Anna and a million questions from us, we wrapped the appointment up and headed to some other appointments within the center.

We traveled to a consultation with anesthesia. Grace Anna had so many things that could possibly go wrong. Besides the shelving in her throat, her spine pressed against her lungs. She was so tiny; this operation would be very taxing on her body.

After a deep discussion of her medical history, the doctors felt she was strong enough to have the surgery. Inside, I was both relieved and anxious by the results. Yes, I wanted her to have this procedure to help her spine, but the thought of what she would face broke my heart.

As the day tarried on, we were getting quite exhausted. An overload of information was given to us, which led to a heap of emotions to deal with throughout the day. It was such a big decision to make, and it would affect the rest of Grace Anna's life. It weighed very heavily on my mind, but Jeff and I knew the doctor was the right person for the surgery.

Surgery was scheduled for January 23. We drove back home the next morning. All five of us were completely drained. Hardly a word was spoken on the ride home. Watching Jeff fight to stay awake, I realized when we returned for the surgery, I would have to get on a plane.

Christmas was full of laughter and joy. We purposely refrained from talking about the surgery during the holidays, but instead focused on the meaning of Christmas and family. I prepared a big meal at our home, and all our families came over to celebrate. It was wonderful to take a break from the realities of life.

After Christmas, I arranged for my absence at school. Jeff also met with his boss at Tarter Farm & Ranch to plan for his absence. We both were very fortunate that our employers readily gave us the time off we needed for Grace Anna's procedure.

Next we needed to plan where we would stay before and after her surgery. I repeatedly went over our finances, trying to come up with the funds for plane tickets and a hotel, but the money wasn't there. I searched the Internet tirelessly, looking for grants and programs.

I connected with an amazing program out of North Carolina called Children's Flight of Hope. Their program provided commercial and private air transportation for specialized health care treatment. After going through their application process, Grace Anna was approved for aid. I was beyond elated—no long, tiresome drive there and back.

Now all I had to do was find accommodations. I reached out to the hospital to discuss whether they might have arrangements with nearby hotels for special rates or discounts. They provided a list of hotels plus some info about a local program where parents could stay in a small facility for parents of patients in the hospital. It was one block away from the hospital and housed fifteen families. We were put on the waiting list until an opening came up. If none came open, we would have to find a hotel nearby.

My good friend Michelle took it upon herself to do a benefit auction for us along with a three-on-three basketball tournament at the Galilean Children's Home. It raised quite a bit of money for Grace Anna's stay at the hospital. We were also very blessed during this time to receive donations from Dunnville Christian Church.

Grace Anna had touched people's hearts from her first moments on this planet. Her unique way of blessing others by just being herself tugged at their hearts. We never asked for help. People were doing it out of the goodness of their hearts. God helps in ways our human minds can't understand at times. People kept asking if they could help. It was a blessing of a great magnitude. We will never forget the kindness we were shown during this time.

Three days before we were to fly out, the phone rang. A spot had opened, and we were now booked in the patient-only facility for up to four weeks. We didn't anticipate staying that long, but the block of time was suggested to make sure we had somewhere in case we needed it.

Grace Anna had to get blood work completed a week prior to her procedure, so we would make a trip out before her surgery then return the following week if everything looked well.

Now, it was time to gather my thoughts and face a fear I had avoided my entire life. I was thirty-nine years old and had never stepped foot on a plane. Whenever I thought about flying, I broke out in a hot flash with sweat dripping from my head to my toes. If I couldn't even think about a plane ride, how was I going to get on one?

"It's just a plane. Thousands fly every day," Jeff would say.

"Yes, and if it goes down, there is a very slim possibility I'll ever make it out of it," I would rebut.

I felt ashamed to be so concerned about the flight, especially when Grace Anna was getting ready to face a major surgery. How could I be such a chicken? Yet, try as I might, each time my mind shifted to thoughts of going up in the air, the oxygen in my body seemed to disappear. I would have to find a way to face this. Grace Anna needed me, and it was ridiculous to be so intimidated by something as simple as riding in a plane.

During my daily prayers, I added a prayer for peace about the plane ride. I would have to allow God to give me peace about the flight. My daughter needed me, and this would more than likely be the first of many flights I would take for her treatment. I had to accept that we would be perfectly fine on a plane.

As we boarded, Grace Anna was all smiles and calm as a cucumber. I also tolerated it well. I wasn't happy Jeff was three rows up from us, but it seemed my nervousness had eased up over the past day. I could do this.

I focused on finding our seats and getting settled. The flight was a short one, so it surely would be tolerable. My real concern was what Grace Anna was getting ready to endure. I fitted her in her car seat within the plane seat and buckled myself in. I grabbed her hand and whispered a soft prayer.

"God, keep us safe, secure, and at peace through the flight. Bless the days ahead and bless my sweet girl. I trust in you."

Takeoff began, and I closed my eyes. I breathed in deeply through my nose and out through my mouth. Grace Anna on the other hand was cackling. The more the altitude climbed, the more she enjoyed it. I caught myself laughing with her. How could it be that something I had been afraid of my entire life was so easy to overcome?

It wasn't me; it was God. He worked through Grace Anna's zest for life to show me how small the fear was and how big He was.

The flight was smooth as silk. I spent most of the time playing with Grace Anna. Before I knew it, we landed and transferred to our next plane. I had spent so much time fearing instead of trusting in God. I could have flown a long time ago, but I allowed fear to get the best of me.

The joy Grace Anna found in a new experience proved to me that life is what we make of it. Whether it be a plane ride or surgery, Grace Anna would find a way to enjoy her life no matter the circumstances. I needed to start doing the same.

We boarded our plane to our final destination, and the flight was as uneventful as the first. I enjoyed looking over the clouds and seeing the landscape as we traveled. It was shocking to me that something I'd feared my entire life was quite relaxing.

When we landed, I was completely surprised to see a beautiful, large, black limo waiting to pick us up. The Children's Flight of Hope program had arranged the limo to take us to our room.

We stayed at a local hotel and rested for the next day. Grace Anna's appointments went very well. We soon headed back to the hotel and prepared for our flight back home.

This time when I flew, the immense fear diminished. We were fortunate to be able to sit with each other. A quick flight to a connecting city then back to Lexington, and we were home.

The next week seemed to fly by. Thank goodness, I had handled all our planning the days before our first trip. I took the week off to allow Grace Anna to enjoy every moment of life she could. I knew the upcoming months were not going to be easy for her to endure.

The day preceding Grace Anna's surgery finally came. We packed up our SUV and headed to a small airport in Junction City. This time we would fly in a small five-passenger plane. It was not quite what I wanted, but once again I reminded myself why we were doing this. Grace Anna was the priority. I tried to let go of my desires and center my thoughts on her life becoming better, not my fears.

The takeoff was quite different than a big plane, but it was not horrible as I expected. Since the flight was a little longer, I had time to pray and relax before facing what would come tomorrow.

God, bless this flight and give our minds peace. Thank you for the guidance and blessings we have received.

I laid my head back and closed my eyes. The world seemed to slow down for a few short hours, so I could be still and breathe. I needed this break to let my mind as well as my body rest.

As we landed, I held Grace Anna's hand and smiled at her. She was grinning from ear to ear. She loved plane rides. As we landed, I noticed this large, black limo waiting for us again. The Children's Flight of Hope knew how to take care of sick children. It was so comfortable and relaxing to sit back in the big limo and enjoy the sights of Baltimore as we traveled to our room.

Once we arrived, the front staff greeted us, went over procedures and policies, then showed us to our room. It was a very nice facility. The staff had dinner for parents every night, and they also helped with necessities like toiletries, laundry, and storage.

We all were ready for a good meal and a good night's rest. We ate with the other families staying at the facility and shared our stories. It was a great moment of bonding with families that shared some of the same struggles we had. For some reason, when you find someone traveling a similar path, it's as if you've known them your entire life.

Even though their children did not have the exact same condition as Grace Anna, their stories of doctors, hospitals, struggles, and experiences created a connection among us. We all were part of a club of sorts: the parents of children with health issues. We lived a different type of life than people with healthy children. We understood each other, and I felt I had found a second family.

Once we finished our food and conversation, we headed to our room. Grace Anna could barely keep her eyes open, and my body ached all over. We needed rest and time to just be our little family.

Grace Anna and I snuggled up in one bed while Jeff took the other. I set the alarm and said my nightly prayer. I leaned over to kiss Grace Anna's head and hold her close to me. "My sweet gal," I softly whispered into her ear, "you are going to be okay."

Within moments we were all asleep, and life was calm.

We had no idea what would come in the days ahead. If we had, we probably would have jumped right back on a plane and headed back to Kentucky. But we didn't know. We can make plans, be courageous, and still be knocked down by events of life. Grace Anna was getting ready to face the fight of her life, and we would understand the complete feeling of helplessness.

5

ALL I CAN DO
IS SING

eep! *Beep! Beep!* The alarm clock blared in my ear. It was surgery day. I jumped out of bed and bolted into the shower. I put on my most comfortable clothes. The surgery would last eight to ten hours, and hospital seats are not known for their comfort.

After I was ready, I woke Jeff up, then dressed Grace Anna. With a big smile on her face, she draped her arms over my shoulders and rested her head against my cheek. Her gentle hug worked like nothing else to made me feel as if life would be all right.

I wrapped her snuggly into her blankets and placed her into her stroller. We exited the room and took the elevator to the first floor. As we walked through the door to the hospital, the sun shone so brightly upon us. I knew in my heart the surgery would be a success.

Jeff quietly walked along beside us. I could tell he was nervous. If I tried to talk to him, the replies were short and to the point. He wasn't in the mood for any deep conversations.

Even though I was positive the surgery would go well, a part of me dreaded what Grace Anna would face once she woke up. Not only were they going to fuse her spine during the surgery, but a neurosurgeon would release a ligament that contributed to her tethered spinal cord.

also wake up to a cast over half of her body. To protect the fusion's stability, it would restrict her bending and twisting her back.

Tears welled up inside me, but I knew I had to remain calm for her. I had been perfecting the art of holding back tears for the past two years. This moment I absolutely needed to be strong and calm for her.

As we entered the hospital, we were directed to the presurgery waiting area. It was full of families with loved ones in surgery. The longer I sat, the more my leg seemed to bounce. I guess you can try your hardest to control your emotions, but sometimes those emotions will be shown through different areas of your body.

Jeff would place his hand on my knee to remind me to relax, but unfortunately for both of us, it wasn't working. I decided to get up and walk. I walked and walked and walked until I released the nervous energy from my body. I couldn't allow this to overcome me. Then a text from my sister rang in.

We're praying, Sis.

It immediately soothed my soul. Then I turned the corner, and there stood my dad and his friend Martha. They had driven all the way here to support Grace Anna and us during surgery and recovery. Dad grabbed me and hugged me tightly. Tears streaming down my face, I whimpered, "I'm so glad you're here, Dad."

We joined Jeff and Grace Anna in the waiting area, anticipating when they would call her back for surgery. Fifteen minutes later, it was time to go. Dad and Martha went down to the postsurgery waiting area while Jeff, Grace Anna, and I headed back to presurgery.

"This is it," Jeff said.

"I know. I'm scared, honey."

"She's tough. She'll be fine."

I wished I could shake the feeling that something wasn't right, but for some reason I felt uneasy all the sudden. I shrugged it off to being a worrywart and kept telling myself she was going pull through the surgery as planned.

The nurse helped get Grace Anna into the gown for surgery. It was now very evident to me that the time was near. Soon, I would hand off my darling to a group of people and trust them to take care of her. It wasn't easy for me to give that duty to someone else. She was my baby.

The doctor soon arrived and marked his initials on her back where he would be operating. Then he went over again the steps he would take and how things would progress throughout the day.

"You will get updates as the surgery progresses," he explained.

"How long do you think it will take?" I asked.

"Anywhere between six to ten hours. It depends on how her bones look once we're in there and how long neurosurgery takes. The cast will be put on after I'm finished in the OR."

We met with the neurosurgeon, anesthesiologist, cast team, and nurses who would be involved in the surgery. They all asked detailed questions about Grace Anna's health. We also comprehensively described the many facets of her medical history.

It was closer to surgery time, so I dressed in scrubs and a mask. I was given the opportunity to carry her back to the operating room and to be with her as they put her under anesthesia.

As I looked down at her angelic face, I trembled. "I love you, sweetheart." I kissed her forehead. She nuzzled up against me, and I breathed in her scent. I wanted to linger there and hold her, but they were waiting on us.

I laid her on the surgery table and held her hand. The mask was placed over her tiny mouth and nose. She stared into my eyes until she could not fight the sedation anymore. She closed her eyes, and her body went limp. I couldn't hold it in anymore. I erupted in tears.

A nurse wrapped her arm around me and escorted me back to Jeff. "She's going to be fine."

I went from crying in a nurse's arm into Jeff's arms. Both of our eyes flooded with tears. It was hard enough to see Grace Anna go off into surgery, but it broke my heart even more to see Jeff cry. He was the strong one, but like me he had held it in as long as he possibly could.

Then from the other side of the room came my dad, in tears too. The only one not crying was Martha. Thankfully one of us kept it together. She directed us to some seats and comforted us until we pulled ourselves together.

I texted the rest of my family and my closest friends that Grace Anna was in surgery. I then posted on Facebook that she was in surgery, and I would update my page when there was any new info. Messages poured in that everyone was praying and thinking of us.

I put my phone on silent and tried to rest. I knew it would more than likely be a long night after she got out of surgery. It was useless. I couldn't relax enough to allow my body to rest. I tried to eat, but food felt like tasteless rocks in my mouth. I ended up grabbing some magazines and a crossword puzzle.

The more difficult the puzzle, the better. Trying to figure out the clues kept Grace Anna off my mind. Crossword puzzles had been something I picked up from my grandma Elma. She always worked them in ink and so did I. When Grandma was upset about something, she could go through twenty crossword puzzles in no time flat.

Just like her, I was flying through the book. I looked up, and three hours had passed. Three hours with no word from the doctors and no idea how the surgery was going. Jeff traveled to the cafeteria to get us some food. I thought about going with him, but I wanted to make sure one of us was there if the doctors came out.

A few bites down, and I was back to trying to distract myself from what was going on with Grace Anna. Between doing crossword puzzles and flipping through magazines, I became incredibly sleepy.

If I shut my eyes for a few moments, surely, I won't miss the doctors.

I had not been asleep very long when a doctor tapped me on the shoulder. "Mrs. Rodgers, I'm assisting the doctor in surgery. Her breathing tube became kinked during surgery. We had to turn her back over to allow them to resolve the problem, so her surgery is running a little behind."

"What? Is she okay?"

"Yes, she is fine. It will put us behind our scheduled time." He went on to explain it would be another three to four hours before they were finished.

I was terrified he was not telling me everything, but all I could do was wait.

Time seemed to drag by. The more minutes that ticked off the clock, the more anxious I became about the outcome of the surgery.

God, please protect her, and let her make it through this.

I couldn't give in to the temptation to break down and panic. I had to remain strong; she would need me when she got out of surgery. I called my sister and updated her on the progress, and she agreed to start calling people to get them praying for her.

Jeff never seemed fazed by anything that was going on during the waiting. He always had complete confidence that the surgical team would follow through and Grace Anna would come out of surgery fine and be ready for home in no time. I loved his confidence, but sometimes it irritated me that he didn't seem concerned when things didn't go as planned. Maybe I was angry at myself for not relying on God and letting the control go.

After a little over ten hours of surgery, the doctor arrived to let us know how our little lady was. "The fusion went fine on its own. There were some problems with anesthesia. She's in the PICU now."

"What happened?" I asked. "Why did the tube kink?"

"I know you had explained to the anesthesia team that a size three intubation tube was recommended by her doctor at Cincinnati Children's Hospital, but they felt a size four would work better. The tube was too large. They had to go back in and replace it with a size three."

I was not happy, to say the least. I don't know if it was because we were just parents or that another hospital's doctor had recommended it, but they didn't listen to us and it did not sit well with me. I decided to address the issue after we saw our Grace Anna.

As I walked into the PICU, my heart sank deep into my chest. Her tiny body was riddled with tubes, too many to count. Monitors beeped as they kept a record of her vital signs, and her little torso was covered in a bright-pink cast. Her face was swollen from the hours of lying on her belly during the surgery. I felt so helpless. What could I do to ease her pain?

I sat down by her bedside, fighting back tears. "Momma's here, honey," I spoke into her ear. I caressed her hand in mine and prayed.

God, please touch Grace Anna. Shield her from pain and fear. Let her know you are here and we are here.

Grace Anna shared a large room with three other children on as many monitors and tubes as Grace Anna. We had very little privacy. Only a curtain separated us from the child next to Grace Anna. A constant beeping continued throughout the day, and alarms went off if a patient's vitals dropped outside the normal level.

Not an environment conducive to rest and quietness, it was centered around ensuring the patients were monitored and taken care of. I understood the need for the equipment and routines, but it was not easy to get an eighteen-month-old little girl to understand everything was safe. I could see in her precious eyes she was afraid.

When she looked at me, I know she wondered why I wouldn't pick her up and comfort her. All the nurses and doctors coming in and out poking and prodding on her body had to be frightening to her, since they were all strangers.

Grace Anna was heavily sedated to keep her calm while recovering from the tethered cord especially. To prevent damage to her spinal cord, she needed to lie flat on her back for three days without twisting or turning. It was a very long three days.

I couldn't pick her up or pat her back, so I did the only thing I thought would comfort her—I sang.

"Amazing grace, how sweet the sound that saved a wretch like me," I softly sang as I looked Grace Anna in the eyes.

For the first time, her eyes eased, so I sang more. I sang every hymn I could remember. As I sang, it felt as if the beeping and constant evaluations became muffled. I felt as if she and I were in a cocoon, sheltered from stimuli that could startle her.

She wrapped her hand gently around my pinkie finger, listening intently to every sound that emitted through my voice. As I sang each song, I felt her body relax and saw in her eyes that she was becoming more at ease with her surroundings.

Once she drifted off to sleep, I would rest my head on her bed right beside her. I didn't want her to wake up to a room full of strangers. Jeff and I would take turns throughout the first night to ensure someone with whom she was familiar was by her side at all times.

My dad and Martha visited for some time and decided to make the long ride back to Baltimore the day after Grace Anna's surgery. For all accounts, Grace Anna was recovering fine and things were going very well.

On the fourth day after her surgery, we were finally able to hold Grace Anna. What happened led to the scariest moments in our lives.

As I took Grace Anna into my arms, something wasn't right. She gasped and tried to say, "Momma," but she couldn't get the words out. Monitors beeped and nurses rushed to her bed.

"What's going on? What's going on?" I yelled at them.

"Ma'am, stand to the side," one of the nurses said.

They assessed Grace Anna's vitals, then I heard, "Her lung has collapsed."

I ran into the waiting room and grabbed Jeff. Running with me, we burst back into the room where a team of medical personnel were working on Grace Anna. They had placed a BiPAP on Grace Anna's mouth and nose. She didn't have her glasses on, and she was crying.

I wanted to rush over to hold her, tell her it was going to be okay, but we couldn't get in. "God, help my baby!" I screamed.

The next few moments were a blur to me. The team worked to get her vitals stable and took X-rays of her lungs. Within an hour we were back by her side holding her hands.

"We're here, Grace Anna. We're here," Jeff and I told her.

She kept looking at us with big tears in her eyes, drifting in and out of sleep. She had been given a sedative to calm her, so she wouldn't fight the BiPAP. The doctor arrived a few moments later to discuss what was going on.

"Her right lung has collapsed. We will supply her with support to breathe and get the fluid out. She's going to be fine. It's going to take some time," he assured us.

I wanted to believe him, but doubt creeped in. Jeff and I were exhausted and on our own. Now neither one of us wanted to leave her side. We felt so alone and had no one there to help. I needed someone there to help. Both of us neared the point of exhaustion and our nerves were frazzled.

I called my sister, Bobbie. "Sis, her lung has collapsed. We need you."

"I don't know how we will do it, but Mom and I will be there as soon as possible," Bobbie said.

As we waited by Grace Anna's side, doctors and nurses monitored her very closely. Her pic line had to be reinserted into her arm, and it seemed like the poking and prodding never ended. I ached for her. I couldn't imagine what she was thinking.

I continued to sing when she awoke and pray when she slept. I sang until I could hardly hold my head up. Nurses urged Jeff and I to go back to our room and rest, but I couldn't leave her side.

The next afternoon my cell phone went off, and I learned that my sister and mom had arrived. Jeff traveled back to our room at the patient facility to get them settled in, but in a very short time they were at the hospital.

Once I saw them, I collapsed into their arms.

"Oh Mom, I don't know what happened. She was fine, then the next thing I know she couldn't breathe."

"It's going to be okay. Sit down and take a breath," she said.

I would love to say once they arrived things became better, but the next day Grace Anna experienced a second event that sent our world spiraling out of our control. Our faith would be tested, and Grace Anna would face the biggest battle of her life. I would continue to sing to my darling every day as she fought to live and prove that she was, in fact, a warrior.

6

A TINY WARRIOR

When the storms of life rage around us, it's hard to see the calm that will come. Grace Anna's right lung had already collapsed, and she fought for every breath she took. With the arrival of my sister and mom, we had family there to support us and her. We had no idea how much we would need that support in the days to come.

Grace Anna had been on the BiPAP machine for three days, yet she had not progressed much toward weaning off it. She couldn't wear her glasses because they wouldn't fit over the nasal mask, so she couldn't see us. There was a constant parade of doctors and nurses in and out of her space.

In a room with three other patients, there's not much privacy or ability to rest. Even if Grace Anna was sedated, she couldn't be completely calm. It was excruciating to watch her lie there terrified and in pain.

"You are so beautiful to me," I sang, laying my head against her side.

A small smile appeared on her face. I held her hand and continued to sing. My singing was one of the few things that would ease her anxiety. All of us began to sing to her when we took our turn sitting with her.

With Bobbie and Mom there, it was the first time Jeff and I could sleep outside of her room. Try as I might, I could not fall asleep in the small sleeping room for parents. I kept worrying Grace Anna would feel alone without one of us there.

How is she? I texted Mom.

She's sleeping. You do the same.

I turned over and started crying into my pillow. I wanted her to get better, and I wanted to go home.

When I awoke early the next morning, I grabbed a cup of coffee and a small bite to eat for Jeff and me. Jeff had spent the night sleeping on a bench in the waiting area. It was like sleeping on a rock, but Jeff didn't complain. He never complained about anything during that time. Grace Anna was his only concern.

We went in to Grace Anna's room. Bobbie rested her head next to my sweet girl's. They both looked so peaceful. I hated to wake Bobbie.

"Sis, we're here. Go back to the room and get some rest," I whispered to her.

Bobbie lifted her head. "I'm going to wait in the waiting room for a while and see how she does when she wakes up."

It had been three days since Grace Anna's lung collapsed. Today they would try removing the BiPAP and letting her use an oxygen cannula, requiring her to do some of the breathing on her own. I was a little nervous to see if she could do it. What would happen if she couldn't?

"Grace will be monitored constantly to see if she can start breathing on her own some," the nurse explained.

That afternoon the cannula was placed and the BiPAP removed. We cautiously waited to see how she would do.

At first she seemed a little scared, but after a few minutes, she became accustomed to breathing on her own. She turned her head toward me and smiled sweetly. Then she reached out, wanting me to take her in my arms. I wanted to hold her so much. I rang for her nurse. I didn't want to do anything that could complicate her recovery.

The nurse asked the doctors if it was okay, and we were green-lighted to hold her. I wanted to jump for joy. Within a few moments, the nurses had situated all her cords, so I could hold her. I was so excited to finally caress my baby girl after such a rough week.

As the nurses helped place Grace Anna in my arms, I bent down to kiss her forehead. She looked back at me, smiling, then started gasping for breath.

"Grace Anna! Grace Anna!"

The nurses pulled her from my arms and back to the bed.

"What is going on?" I asked. "Why isn't she breathing?"

Jeff stood on the other side of the bed yelling, "What is wrong with her?"

No one would answer us, but they continued to work on her. The longer they worked, the clearer it became that they couldn't get her to breathe. I ran to get my mom and sister in the waiting room.

"She's not breathing!

"What?" Mom asked.

"Pray for her! Please pray."

I ran back to the room, but the nurses wouldn't let Jeff or me in. Jeff wouldn't take no for answer. He burst his way through the nurses and stood five feet from Grace Anna's bed.

"If you stand right here, you can stay. Just don't go any closer. They are trying to help her," a nurse insisted.

Jeff stood in silence, watching as they repeatedly tried to put a breathing tube down Grace Anna's throat without success. I couldn't take it anymore. I couldn't watch my baby girl take her last breath. I ran as fast as I could. I couldn't breathe. I fell to my knees in the waiting room. *Please, God! Please don't take her. I can't live without her.*

My mom and sister gathered around me, praying and crying. A code blue was issued, and we watched a second set of doctors rush into her room. It felt as if I was watching from outside my body. I couldn't feel my skin anymore. The world seemed like a dream in extremely slow motion.

My sister worked the phone, telling everyone to pray. "She's a fighter. She's going to make it. Just believe."

Time seemed to slow to a lull. I was so numb I couldn't speak or think of what to say. Then Jeff came around the corner.

"They saved her," he said. "She's okay."

Jeff fell into my arms and wept, his entire body shaking. My crying turned more into a moaning, so thankful God guided the doctors.

One of the doctors on call pulled us to the side and explained, "Both of her lungs are now collapsed. Her throat is swollen from the complications with anesthesia during surgery. The shelving in her throat also caused issues with finding the right breathing tube. We had to put in a different type of tube. She is on the BiPAP, and we will have to take it day by day."

Each day Grace Anna proved to be the warrior we all knew she was, enduring endless tests and examinations. She continued to fight for her life. Doctors had to give her higher doses of sedation due to her fighting so hard to take the BiPAP machine off. She wanted free so desperately, and she couldn't understand that what was scaring her was helping her.

I continued to sing and pray over her. My mom and sister helped us by switching out shifts of sitting with her so Jeff and I could eat and sleep. I don't know what we would have done without the two of them. They not only helped us rest; they kept us from losing our minds.

We also became very acquainted with a host of other families basically living in the hospital with us, sharing our favorite stories of home and our families. It was a very diverse group from New Jersey all the way down to Florida—all of us there with our children, weathering our own battles.

Those families became part of our family. When you share a tight space with people going through similar battles, special bonds form. They saw us at our worst and held our hands through some tough days. We may have lived very different lives at home, but in those days, our lives were the same.

Our hometown sent care packages, letters, prayers cloths, and financial support in the days we waited, aching for the moment we knew Grace Anna would be out of the woods.

I took the prayer cloths and placed them at the foot of her bed, thinking they would be like guardian angels over her. After a few days, Grace Anna slowly improved but then started running a fever.

"We are going to run some tests to see if there is an infection somewhere in her body," the doctor explained.

The tests showed Grace Anna did not have an infection. Doctors were stumped about why she kept running a fever. My mom knew.

"She's overheating because of the cast," Mom explained. "She's always gotten hot so easily."

At first the doctors dismissed the idea, but a knowledgeable nurse listened. Within moments he and Mom had put an oxygen tube down Grace Anna's cast. Sure enough, within minutes her fever started to drop.

"That is amazing," the doctor said. "I would never have thought the cast would have caused that."

Her scarring from ichthyosis made her unable to regulate her body temperature effectively. With the cool air traveling through her cast, the temperature came down. Nanny Kathy knew what she was talking about and persisted until someone listened. I learned from her that day that even when doctors tell you it can't be, they can be wrong. If something continues to pull at you, there is a reason. God is trying to get your attention.

After twenty-two days in the hospital, Grace Anna was progressing to hopefully removing the BiPAP and getting out of PICU. Her X-rays looked clear, so the doctors ordered the removal of the BiPAP. The cannula was to be placed. I sure was hoping the cannula placement would go much smoother than before.

The nurses carefully removed the BiPAP machine and placed the cannula. I held my breath and prayed for the best. Jeff was standing right over the nurses' shoulders, watching every move they made. Once in, we all stood back and waited for her to show us that warrior spirit. She began to breathe and smile. We placed her glasses back on her, and she could see us for the first time in all those days since her first lung collapsed. I wanted to hold Grace Anna, but this time I decided to wait until we knew for sure she would be okay.

For the rest of the day, Jeff and I never left her side, watching and waiting. As night fell, we both realized our tiny warrior would make it this time. She fell asleep listening to some of my favorite gospel songs. As she gently closed her eyes, Jeff looked over at me. "She's gonna make it," he said. "I think we can breathe now too."

Tears streamed down my face, and I hugged him tightly. I could not imagine anyone else I could have faced the last month with other than Jeff. He was a rock the entire time, while I broke down during the scariest episodes in our lives. I knew he was exhausted.

"Go back to the room and rest. She's going to be fine," I insisted.

Jeff headed down the hallway, while Bobbie and Mom remained by my side.

"I think you two can go home. They need you there," I added.

After some discussion, Bobbie would go home the following day, but Mom insisted on staying a few more days until Grace Anna was out of the PICU.

Grace Anna improved greatly overnight, and the next morning I held my sweet girl.

"Oh girl, I've missed this," I said, caressing her in my arms. "I'm never letting you go."

Grace Anna laid her head on my shoulder. Big tears rolled down her cheeks. She didn't have to say anything. I knew she finally felt safe. As I rocked her back and forth in my arms, I softly whispered, "Thank you, Lord. Thank you."

After two more days, her cannula was removed, and Grace Anna was moved from the PICU to a room with seven other patients. It wasn't ideal. The hospital needed some updates. Water flooded the bathroom, which was overcrowded and lacked privacy. We had to make do with what was available, and we hoped she would be out of there soon.

Grace Anna hadn't eaten anything since her first lung collapsed. I knew she had to be hungry.

"Can I feed her?" I asked.

"You might want to try feeding her something gentle the first few days," the nurse suggested.

They didn't know Grace Anna very well. By the end of the conversation, she had scarfed down a chocolate pudding and was asking for more. The tiny warrior still had a warrior's appetite and needed more food. She continued to eat until her belly was full, and then she drifted off to sleep.

One night on the floor, and the doctor said we could stay at the patient facility for a couple of days. The longer she stayed in the hospital, the longer she could develop an infection. It was music to our ears. We wanted out of the hospital!

More than simply the conditions of the hospital bothered us. Many of the children did not have parents with them for whatever reason, and we listened to one of them cry all night for his momma. It was heart-wrenching not being able to comfort him.

The next three days, we stayed at the facility. Then, after a quick checkup, we headed home. This had been the roughest time in our lives, especially for Grace Anna. I had watched my daughter fight for almost a month to breathe and stay in this world, aching for the day she would be ready for me to hold her. That experience would change how we did things from then on.

I couldn't wait to get back home to Isaiah. He had been staying with my sister's family while we were gone. I looked forward to sleeping in our bed and seeing Grace Anna resting peacefully, safe and secure at home. We were so blessed that she made it through the surgery and recovery.

The next year, Cincinnati Children's Hospital received a very large donation. This turned their old, run-down hospital into a state-of-the-art facility that would give each child a private ICU room and amazing accommodations for families. It was a greatly needed improvement.

I wish I could say all the friends we made through Grace Anna's hospital stay could've had the same positive results as us.

Unfortunately, one family we became very close with never had the chance to bring their son home. He died at the hospital. Our hearts broke for them. It forever changed their lives and made us much more aware of how fortunate we were to bring Grace Anna home.

Seeing so many children without family in the hospital weighed on our minds. I ached for them, knowing they were facing health challenges like Grace Anna had, but without someone there who loved them. I couldn't understand why things had to be that way, and I prayed God would comfort them.

In almost a month at the hospital, our lives dramatically changed. We almost lost Grace Anna, and our world was turned upside down. Through the support of our family, community, good doctors, good nurses, and God's healing touch, Grace Anna made it home. Life became more about family and less about the trivial things in life. We had been given a second chance with our daughter. We were not going to waste it.

Grace Anna would continue to see her doctor the next three years for checkups, a therapy stay, and a successful insertion of a metal rod for her growing body. Unfortunately, life circumstances would cause an abrupt change in who her spine doctor would be in the future, creating a stressful decision for our family once again.

God had big plans for Grace Anna. That mountain she just climbed would prepare her to become a light to the world. Our tiny warrior was getting ready to take the world by storm after facing her own. Hang on, world, here comes Grace Anna!

7

HEARING IS BELIEVING

Once we settled in at home, we desperately needed life to take on some resemblance of normal. I've learned, however, when you have a child with health issues, surprising events become the new normal.

Some of the things I loved to do before I had Grace Anna I could not do now, and that was okay. My prayer of having another child was answered, and I would not be selfish because raising her wasn't what I had envisioned. God gave Grace Anna to me for a purpose. She suffered pains I never experienced. What kind of mother would I be if I was upset because I had to give up things that used to be important to me?

Grace Anna's cast took quite a bit of adjusting to—not just for her, but for all of us. I couldn't pick her up and hold her as I used to. Snuggling was a balancing act. I would place one of my hands on the side of her thigh and the other arm up underneath her shoulders with her body leaning against my chest. Picking her up with direct pressure pushing up against her bottom was unsafe due to the pressure put on her spine during recovery.

Her underarms became irritated due to the cast, and her poor little body seemed to overheat so easily in it. I found myself spending most days trying to make her comfortable. On summer and spring days when most people enjoyed the weather in pools or at the lake, we stayed inside. Sometimes I felt very isolated in our home. Many days we didn't have visitors. People were busy living their own lives. Most days it was Grace Anna and me, which was okay.

"All right, little lady, what is it going to be today?" I asked Grace Anna.

She wasn't verbal enough yet to express exactly what she wanted, so I tried several things to soothe her and bring her some relaxation. I read book upon book, we watched episodes of her favorite television shows, *Sesame Street* and *Peppa Pig*, and we rocked in the rocking chair while listening to our favorite music.

Grace Anna couldn't maneuver around our home as she had prior to the surgery. She had never crawled like most young children, but she would army-crawl, pulling her legs behind her. With the cast, she could barely make it from one side of the room to the other.

One day she was trying her best to cross the room, and she couldn't muster enough energy to get there to play with some toys. Frustrated, she pushed her arms forward trying to propel herself to the other side of the room. Next thing I knew, she was spinning like a top.

I raced to her side. "Grace Anna, what are you doing? Are you hurt?"

She never opened her mouth. She became quiet. I repeated her name, but she refused to reply. Her face turned extremely red, and her eyes grew as big as saucers. "Honey, please say something to Momma."

She never spoke, never looked at me or acknowledged I was trying to get her attention. What happened next was very unexpected but proved once again, Grace Anna can make a bad situation better just by being herself.

"Weeeeeeeee!" she howled. "Weeeeeeeeeee!"

By balancing the cast in a certain way, she'd become a human spinning top. She threw her hands in the air. At first it terrified me; I was concerned it would put pressure on her spine. I tried to get her to slow down, but the more I asked her to, the faster she spun.

To be on the safe side, I called her surgeon.

He assured me the cast would protect her and told me, "If she can do it on her own, she will be fine. As long as you are not forcing her body to do something, the cast will keep her spine protected and it will heal fine."

"Thanks so much," I replied. "At least she's having some fun."

When I got off the phone, she spun so fast I could barely stand to watch. Yet, her uncontrollable laughter was a sight to see. Her little arms became incredibly strong while she was in the cast. She used them to go wherever she wanted to. Even though this heavy cast lay on her back, it did not stop her will to live her life under her own terms.

Besides the occasional trip to my sister's or my mom's, we spent many days at home. We did go to church some, but it was so hard to find clothing to fit over the cast. It was even more difficult to sit at church comfortably, especially if it was the least bit hot. If Grace Anna started to get too hot, she panicked.

I started packing an insulated bag with cool, damp rags in case she became hot. We would place them around her neck, making sure they didn't get her cast damp. I strove to balance making sure she was healthy physically, mentally, and socially. Grace Anna has always loved people, so giving her opportunities to interact with others besides me was very important.

It was hard at times to find children her age to interact with. I was an older mom and most people my age didn't have children Grace Anna's age. The young children in my family lived quite a distance away. Many days Grace Anna spent with adults or teenagers. My nephew Nate was the youngest that visited at age eleven. He was so wonderful with Grace Anna, as well as my niece Myla. They both gave her the personal connection she needed from someone besides me.

With all my planning and problem-solving to help Grace Anna, I had become exhausted. I wanted to do everything I could to help her, but my body told me I needed to slow down. Recently diagnosed with hypothyroidism on top of what doctors thought was fibromyalgia, I had to realize I could only do what my body would let me. To take care of Grace Anna, I had to take care of myself.

All my life I've been in love with music, and Grace Anna loved it too. I've always been a big fan of all types of music if it didn't have vulgarity in it. My dad used to sit on my childhood home's front porch and sing bluegrass music to me. He played his guitar and banjo so effortlessly; it was something I treasured from my childhood.

Those memories sparked something in me as I sat with Grace Anna each day. When we rocked in the rocking chair, I sang to her. When I bathed her, I sang to her. If I wasn't eating or sleeping, most of the time I would be singing. At times, it drove Jeff crazy.

"Angie, I'm trying to watch television," he would say. "Can you tone it down?"

I didn't even realize I was singing.

Grace Anna was by my side much of the day, so she heard me singing and humming. It was like she was studying my lips at times, trying to learn exactly how I was making all those sounds. Her little feet would kick and her arms would dance as she listened to me belt out each song.

At night, I would lay her beside me in bed and sing one of my favorite old-time lullabies.

"Oh be oh by oh baby oh be oh by of mine, oh be oh by oh baby, oh be oh by of mine," I would softly sing as she stared intently at my eyes. At times, she would sway with the music as if it were overtaking her body. She seemed to be at one with the music, allowing it to move her spirit.

Then it happened.

"Oh be oh by oh baby oh be oh by of mine, oh be oh by oh baby, oh be oh by of mine," Grace Anna sang it as pure and beautiful as I had ever heard.

Then she continued to her next song.

"Amazing grace, how sweet the sound, that saved a wretch like me. I once was lost, but now I'm found, was blind, but now I see," she sang without missing a beat.

I lay there astonished by what I heard. How could a little girl who could barely form a three-world sentence be able to sing like this? Astonished at how well she knew the words, I was even more amazed by how well she sang. Unlike most sixteen-month-old children, she already had bravado in her voice.

She continued to sing many of the songs I randomly sang throughout the day. I've always considered myself a decent singer, but Grace Anna's voice was something special. Her body reacted incredibly to the sound coming out of her tiny mouth. She trembled as if the joy created by the music came out of every part of her body. I listened to her in awe.

"Grace Anna, that is amazing."

She continued to sing, staring deeply into my eyes. Her song healed some of the hurt I'd experienced the past two years from all the miscarriages. I realized God saved this special girl to not only heal me but for a special purpose. It was no accident she had this voice along with her health struggles. I knew at that moment God had a big plan for her. I didn't know how big that plan was at the time.

The next day I called every family member who would listen to me. I'm sure they thought I was nuts, but in time they witnessed for themselves how talented she was.

My mom stayed with Grace Anna when I had to run errands. She had also been singing with her. "I knew she could do it. She wasn't just listening to us sing; she was figuring out how to do it herself."

As the days at home progressed, we kept singing. My solos turned into duets with Grace Anna, and before long she sang while I worked around the house. At times, I'm positive Jeff and Isaiah thought they were in a musical.

At night, we sang to each other. It was pure magic. I no longer thought about what we were missing or the heartaches of the past. I was lost in two of my favorite parts of life: Grace Anna and music. We sang old-time bluegrass songs or pop music. Whatever we felt in our souls we sang.

There were times I lay in bed listening to her sing. Her singing changed how she dealt with the pain of being in a cast. She would not allow life's hurdles to take over. She would enjoy life no matter the circumstances.

With all she had been through in her very short life, she had been a great teacher to me. Life is not always wonderful. Hurdles and obstacles come. How we handle those hurdles and obstacles define who we are and who we become. This petite wonder was showing me how to dig deep to live fearlessly and walk in joy, no matter what life threw at me.

As the months progressed, Grace Anna's voice became richer and her song catalog grew vaster. She moved from traditional children songs and hymns to artists like Mercy Me and Natalie Grant. She seemed to absorb any music played around her. If there was music, she was happy.

The bond between us became stronger due to the time and love between us and the music. God had blessed Grace Anna with an incredible gift for music. It tickled my spirit to know my daughter loved music as much as I did. She had something I didn't have though—a calling. Her voice would do great things for people. I knew it.

With the adaptions to the cast, life was getting easier to navigate. Grace Anna was restoring my belief that life had good things to offer if we opened our eyes to it. God used Grace Anna to heal the hurt of losing my babies, but I was not yet ready to let go of one child. A child few knew about, but one I could never let go of.

At the time, I couldn't imagine letting go of a hurt I'd carried for over twenty years. God knew with my daughter's help, I would finally be able to move on.

8

BUSY AS A BEE

As time moves on, some days you remember vividly and some seem like a blur. With Grace Anna, we spent so many days in and out of doctors' offices, therapy rooms, and hospitals that at times I could have met myself on the road.

By the time Grace Anna was two years old, she saw eight doctors on a regular basis stretched out over three states. She traveled for occupational and physical therapies as well as checkups. I attempted to continue teaching while keeping her at all her appointments. I constructed a binder that went wherever we went to help keep me organized through the hectic days. It was quite stressful at times.

"Ma'am," the nurse said. "The doctor will see her now."

"Oh my goodness, I'm so sorry. I must have fallen asleep."

Jeff had slipped off to the restroom while Grace Anna and I napped in the waiting room.

It had been a very long day at Cincinnati Children's Hospital. Grace Anna saw several doctors in a day, so we wouldn't have to make the three-and-a-half-hour trip several times a month. It made for long days, but it kept me from using all my sick days.

Grace Anna handled those days much better than I did. As usual, she had a smile on her face everywhere we went. The long days didn't seem to faze her; neither did the long rides.

Dr. Motley, her ophthalmologist, was her first doctor for the day. Things went like clockwork. One of the wonderful things about Cincinnati Children's Hospital is that the different departments all work together for the good of the child. If one doctor is running behind, a call is made to the next appointment preparing to switch things around so the patient can still make all appointments.

Dr. Motley had always been one of our favorite doctors. "Good morning," he said as he shook my hand. "How are you doing, Grace Anna?"

"Good," Grace Anna replied.

Even though Grace Anna wasn't talking enough yet to carry on a very intense conversation, Dr. Motley included her in the conversation every time we saw him. I loved that about him. Everything was happening to her. I appreciated that he realized that.

We had encountered doctors who never spoke to Grace Anna. It was frustrating to her and infuriated me. We did not stay with those types of doctors. God gives us the unction about decisions and many times we tend to ignore them. The first few times I got that knot in my stomach about a doctor I ignored it, but after living through the consequences, I learned to listen to God and quit trying to solve everything on my own.

One thing Grace Anna did not like about seeing Dr. Motley was the pressure check. I can't say that I blamed her. I don't know how well I would handle an odd-looking, clicking instrument coming at my eye.

Try as we might to work together to get it done, she would fight her way out of it almost every time. He would get a reading, but many times she was so stressed it wouldn't be very accurate. After a while we decided Dr. Motley could do a quick pressure check and eye exam while she was sedated for a minor procedure.

The appointment went very well, and we were on our way to her second appointment with Dr. Rutter.

As we made our way across the hospital to the next office, I watched Jeff push Grace Anna down the hall in her stroller. He had become such a good daddy. I was so thankful he made all the out-of-state trips with us. I could've made the trips on my own, but it was better with him along.

When we arrived at Dr. Rutter's office, it was bursting with patients. I expected a bit of a wait, which was fine with us. We could catch a short nap in between appointments.

Then I saw her.

A beautiful little brunette girl, laughing and full of life and wonder. I watched her profile looking up at a woman who appeared to be her mother. The love between them was obvious. The mother doted on her, and the little girl responded with great adoration.

Their interaction reminded me of Grace Anna and myself. We had become so close through all her trials that we were more than mother and daughter. I don't have the words to describe it. It's a feeling, a bond that forms, stronger than any human relationship I have experienced.

As I watched them, I wondered if this mother had been through things like we had. Had they experienced the long stays in hospitals, countless doctors' appointments, choosing which doctors to care for her daughter, and the uncertainty of what tomorrow might bring?

Then the little girl turned around, and I immediately knew: her daughter had more than likely experienced the same if not more trials than our Grace Anna. I pushed down my urge to cry. I had to respect the feelings of this little girl and her momma.

When the little girl turned around, half of her beautiful face was a massive tumor. She was missing half of her mouth, half of her nose, and one of her eyes. Suddenly Grace Anna's condition didn't seem as dire as it had a few moments earlier.

As I continued to watch them play, the little girl remained full of joy as did the mother. The longer I watched, the more I wondered if they had much support at home. Were people kind to them? Did she deal with health issues besides the tumor? Was the little girl in pain?

I never tried to interfere with their day. Who was I to invade their privacy? But that moment changed me. I knew then, even though we had experienced some very hard days, we still needed to give back to others as our great community had when Grace Anna was in such a dire way.

I looked at Grace Anna all comfortable in her daddy's arms, and I felt such an overwhelming need to pick her up and hold her close to me, but once again, that was about me. She needed to rest. I settled my head on Jeff's shoulder and waited for the nurse to arrive.

"Grace Anna Rodgers," the nurse called.

"That's us." I grabbed the stroller, and Jeff carried Grace Anna back to her room.

Dr. Rutter is a native New Zealander and extremely witty. His dry humor didn't always resonate with Grace Anna, but his lovely accent did. She would giggle generously as soon as he started talking to her. He too involved Grace Anna in her care. He talked to her just like he did us.

Grace Anna had some hearing issues early on; she struggled to hear high frequencies in her right ear, which made her singing so much more amazing to me. She had already had one set of ear tubes, so we were hoping this time we could avoid another set.

"Grace Anna, let's take a look-see in those ears of yours."

Grace Anna fidgeted in my lap. She did not like anyone looking in her ears, but Dr. Rutter had a way of talking her into allowing him to peek in.

"All righty then, I believe we've got it," he said. "Grace Anna, you have become quite boring."

"Boring?" Jeff asked.

"Oh, Grace Anna is not boring, but her ears have become boring, which is a good thing," he clarified.

It was hilarious to watch the interactions between Jeff, Grace Anna, and Dr. Rutter. If her ears were boring, it meant no more tubes, and I couldn't be happier about it.

As the appointment neared a closing, we scheduled a follow-up appointment for five months, one of the longest breaks Grace Anna had in between visits. It was a very successful appointment.

Even though Grace Anna had received such a wonderful report, the little girl from earlier in the day weighed heavily on my mind.

I wondered how her appointment went, how she would spend the rest of her day, and most importantly: was she okay?

As we walked down the halls of the hospital, I noticed the children we encountered: children facing incredible battles at such a very young age; children with tubes, monitors, in wheelchairs, in wagons; children fighting for a day of feeling well.

Who was with those children? Their families. Families like us, who were living each day, and at times each moment, the best way they possibly could. How was it fair that these children and families had to live like this?

Then my chest tightened, and I felt as if my lungs wouldn't work. I sweated profusely, and everything became incredibly loud. What was wrong with me?

"Jeff, I have to get outside."

"What's wrong?"

"I don't know. I can't breathe."

Once outside, I started weeping. I didn't know what was going on. Jeff stood by my side, rubbing my back. "Take some deep breaths." He tried to comfort me. "I think you're having a panic attack."

Within a few minutes of concentrating on Jeff's voice and my breathing, my breathing returned to normal and my body calmed down. "You're right. It was a panic attack. I guess I don't understand why Grace Anna and all these other kids have to go through what they do. There has to be something we can do to help."

"I know, honey, but we're not superheroes. We can barely take care of Grace Anna," Jeff replied. "Let's talk about this later, after we get home."

Grace Anna always seemed so at ease, but right then she wasn't. She was worried about me, and I felt very guilty causing her any more grief than she already had. I knelt down beside her. "Grace Anna, I'm so sorry. Momma is fine. We will plan a fun day tomorrow."

She bent over, rubbed my face, and smiled. She comforted me when she most undoubtedly needed comfort. I had to pull it together, let go of questioning things, and refocus on how I could help my family and others.

One more appointment to go, and we could start our way back to Kentucky. It would be a quick stop to the lab so Grace Anna could get some blood work performed. For a two-year-old little girl, she handled it quite well. We were in and out in fifteen minutes without her shedding a tear.

After a five-hour visit to doctors and labs, we could finally load up and head home. The long drive home gave me plenty of time to brainstorm ideas about how we could help other families.

Once we grabbed a quick bite to eat at a local drive-through, we were on our way. Grace Anna was fast asleep within a few minutes; the day had worn her out. I began writing ideas of what helped most.

Prayers topped the list, followed by visiting, but we already prayed for families, and it would be incredibly hard to drag Grace Anna to visit others when she faced major health concerns of her own.

Then it hit me. When Grace Anna spent those many days in the hospital after her first surgery, the care packages greatly lifted our load and brightened our days. We had received six boxes full of snacks, cards, magazines, and essentials that would help us while we were living away from home.

That was it—a charity to help families during long hospital stays. But what would I call it and who could we do it for?

Once home, I fed Grace Anna supper, gave her a bath, and rocked her to sleep. The long trips always wore her out. It wasn't very hard to convince her to go to bed those days. Once she was asleep, I discussed my ideas with Jeff and Isaiah.

"How are you going find out who needs it?" Isaiah asked.

"I think we could get referrals from people in the community," I explained. "People want to help. They just don't know how to get it together. We could take donations, get them together, and deliver to families."

"That's a great idea," Jeff added.

"I'll help," Isaiah chimed in.

Their involvement made it even better. Now we had to come up with a name and decide what we would include. I bounced ideas around, but the one that really stuck with me was naming it after my two children. Using their nicknames, Gracie for Grace Anna and Bug for Isaiah, we came up with Graciebug Bundles of Love.

We decided to include neccessities that would last a while, such as snacks, drinks, magazines, soap, shampoo, socks, pens, toothpaste, toothbrushes, and other essentials. We also wanted to bring joy to children during their hospital stay, so we decided to include items the children would love. This would take finding out their favorite things from the families.

We were all set. We started posting about it on Facebook, and within one week, we had our first referral from my friend Susan.

Susan introduced me to her friend, Julie. After talking with Julie, she told me about her daughter who was battling a rare disorder called ataxia-telangiectasia, which caused her body to progressively lose muscle control, suffer immune system problems, and incur a high rate of cancer. Madeline had been a very active girl, then at the age of eight, she started having balance problems, which led to the diagnosis. By ten she was confined to a wheelchair. Then at fourteen she battled a type of cancer called diffuse large B-cell lymphoma. Her story inspired me so much. This family needed something to make their lives a little more enjoyable.

After finding out some things Madeline liked, we created a Graciebug Bundle to deliver to her hospital room. It included a personalized blanket, all kinds of edible goodies, bubbles, magazines, and other items tailored to what she and her family could use and liked.

The day arrived when we would drop it off at Cincinnati Children's Hospital. I was rather nervous about it. I wanted to make sure whatever I delivered did exactly what we wanted it to do: make their lives easier and happier.

I explained to Grace Anna, "I'm going to deliver this to a girl that is very sick. Because you are so young, you will stay here with Daddy."

"Okay, Momma," she happily replied.

I walked down the hallways to Building A where Madeline's room was. Doctors were very selective about who they allowed in the room with her. To protect her already fragile immune system, no one who had been sick or around someone who had been sick could enter the room

In my head, I pictured making a difference in their lives. I had this great plan of how I would influence her, but when I entered the room, my plan escaped my mind. This beautiful young girl had lost most of her hair, was very thin, and battled a very destructive disease. It was nothing like what I had imagined.

Madeline was very sick, but her spirit was the type of which great stories are told. She had no self-pity. She didn't complain. She was full of spunk and grit. Although the disease had taken a toll on her body, her spirit remained on fire and full of life. Not a beaten-down soul, she spoke her mind and was a very strong-willed young woman. She wasn't allowing the cards life had dealt her to block her from being who she was. She was brilliant.

Madeline was not shy either. I felt honored as she described her health battles and the joys she still found in life. Like most girls her age, she talked of her friends, music, and her family, but one big difference was how she inspired others. By simply being herself, she proved that no matter what life hurls at you, you can be a light in the middle of a raging storm.

During the time I spent with Madeline and Julie, I realized what warriors they both were. A great mom, Julie did whatever her sick child needed. Madeline's courage, facing something most adults could not face, made me want to live my life fearlessly. Her warm, inviting spirit made my heart ache that she was living in a hospital. Most girls her age were taking dance classes, playing sports, or hanging out with their friends having fun.

I was also drawn to the bond between Madeline and Julie. They obviously loved each other with every fiber in their body. Julie didn't treat Madeline like she was an unfortunate soul but with respect and guidance, offering ideas for Madeline and allowing her to decide as much of her life as she possibly could. The level of strength it took Julie to watch her daughter face the daily struggles without breaking down filled me with a newfound strength of my own. I was in complete awe of how the two of them had taken a very tough situation and shaped their lives into something meaningful and full of hope.

It seemed so unfair that this brilliant girl was suffering while I was so healthy. She was just a kid. Why did this all happen? I couldn't answer that, but I could try my best to do something to ease her pain in some way, even if it was just supplying her with bubbles in her hospital room.

I'd never met anyone like Madeline. Not angry or bitter, she lived every moment to the fullest her body would allow. The admiration I felt for Madeline and Julie built a renewed fire in my spirit to be a warrior for Grace Anna and other children. I knew after I met them, I had more I needed to do to make the lives of children with health issues and disabilities better.

I left her room and made it down the halls back to Grace Anna and Jeff. I wanted to cry but felt very selfish in doing so. Why was I crying? Madeline was the one suffering. I needed to do whatever I could to help children like her, children like Grace Anna, the best I could through our charity.

"How did it go?" Jeff asked.

"She was incredible," I told him. "Their strength is indescribable."

"Are you okay?"

"I'm fine. We need to continue helping families. People did it for us. We can do something, even if it is a few families a year. We can make a difference for someone."

He agreed. We pulled out of the parking lot and headed once again back to Kentucky.

I spoke with Madeline's mom a few times throughout the years, keeping updated on how she was doing. On April 28, 2014, Madeline took her last breath at home and went on to be with our Lord.

Her life made such an impact on her family, and we never would have met her if Grace Anna hadn't come into our lives. God has incredible ways of bringing people together. He took two fearless girls to impact the lives of so very many people.

I never saw the little girl from the waiting room that catapulted me into forming our charity. I wish I had. I would love to tell her and her momma what a difference their relationship had on me. I changed after I saw them that day. I would also like for them to meet Grace Anna. I know they would have so much in common. I wished they knew the love they showed each other that day made us better people.

Grace Anna's life changed how we spent our days. Her health battles also opened our eyes to how other children were suffering. The encounters I had with children battling health issues while Grace Anna was climbing her own health mountains changed the woman I was. God showed me that many children face terrible fights with their health, and I could help them in my own little way. Even though it wasn't a large endeavor, Graciebug Bundles of Love made us a better family and helped us make things better for other families.

Grace Anna's sweet spirit had influenced me to be better, do something, and live in the moment. She never allowed her health to ruin her day or cause her to lose her joy. Through a song our family cherished, this great joy in her heart would later inspire people to live happily no matter what was going on in their lives.

9

DADDY'S GIRL

My husband, Jeff, grew up an only child to older parents. What is even more unique is that he was an only grandchild on both sides of his family. When we met, he was quite spoiled; well, he was spoiled rotten.

Even though he had been catered to quite a bit growing up, he had a very strong work ethic and a very big heart. He just didn't like to show it much. The first time he and Isaiah met was probably one of the most awkward moments I've witnessed in my life.

Jeff hadn't been around children much, and it showed. Getting him to understand how to relate to Isaiah frustrated me at times. He often felt Isaiah should function like a little adult. There were times I questioned whether our relationship would work. I had made it abundantly clear that Isaiah was my priority. If he couldn't have a good relationship with him, he couldn't have a good relationship with me.

"Honey, I look at it like a science experiment. If something doesn't work with you two, I try something different," he explained.

"We're not a science experiment," I replied. "You're going to have to start letting your walls down."

He didn't like that. It made him extremely uncomfortable to let his guard down and allow someone to care about him. It was even harder for him to express how he felt about us. Isaiah and I were very outspoken with our affection for each other. We laughed, cut up, hugged each other, and talked all the time. Jeff was more the silent type.

His sense of humor was very dry, and at times I wondered if he had any emotions. This is perhaps why we dated for quite a while before we married. I had been through one divorce. I was not going to go through another one. I cared about him, but I needed someone who could love Isaiah and me wholeheartedly without limits.

Each day a little more of Jeff's inner self opened up to us. He began to joke around and show us a different side of himself. We did things all together—things he liked to do, Isaiah's multiple ball games and events, and things I enjoyed. We were coming together as a family unit. It wasn't long before Jeff asked me to marry him, and we became husband and wife.

In the first two years of our marriage, there was quite a bit of adapting. We had suffered so much loss after the death of Jeff's dad and the miscarriages. There were many days we lived in survival mode. Survival mode for Jeff meant holding everything in and not showing he was hurting.

All of this pushed-down pain manifested itself at night during his sleep.

"What are you doing?" I asked.

"There's something in the bed. Get up!" Jeff yelled as he threw the blanket off me.

His sleepwalking became such a big problem early in our marriage that he went to a family physician to seek help. Doctors could not fix what was wrong with him. He had to start opening up to us and realizing it was okay if he was not the strong one all the time.

The more my pregnancy with Grace Anna progressed, the less Jeff walked in his sleep. The bigger my belly grew, the lighter his spirit became. The hope of her arrival was slowly transforming him back into the man he was before tragedy struck our family.

Once Grace Anna arrived, the man I knew disappeared. He was replaced with a gooey, mushy man who was also solid as a rock. Grace Anna brought a side to him I had never witnessed. I was grateful for it.

Before Grace Anna was born, he often felt nervous around

newborns and toddlers, because he was unsure how to take care of them. After she was born, he became a natural. He bathed her, fed her, and took care of her *almost* as good as me. (I'll never admit he was actually as good as I was.)

One evening he grew tired of his goatee and shaved it off. He waltzed into the living room and the laughter began.

"Grace Anna, what is so funny?" he asked.

All she could do was cackle. Every time he smiled, she would light up like a Christmas tree. It was an evening of him making silly faces and her rubbing his cheeks and chin, then bursting into laughter. When I thought they couldn't laugh anymore, it would start over again.

He took the time each evening to spend moments with just the two of them. Whether he read to her or watched a cartoon, they sat down together and had their daddy and daughter time.

Then came the times when his heart broke because of what she faced.

One morning I was cleaning the kitchen when the phone rang.

"What are you doing?" he asked.

"Sweeping."

"Can you go somewhere you'll be alone."

I agreed and immediately become concerned. "What is it? Something wrong at work? Are you sick?" I rattled off, not giving him a chance to reply.

"Honey, when I put Grace Anna to bed last night, we were playing, and I told Grace Anna I was going to steal her feet. She turned to me with eyes big as saucers and told me she needed her feet, because she was going to walk someday." He began to sob.

I wept profusely, so much I couldn't utter a word. When she hoped for things she couldn't do, which many kids do very easily, I would break down.

"I can't get it off my mind," he said, crying. "I just want to see her do it. She wants it so desperately."

"We must do everything in our power to make it happen, give

her every tool, and support her each step of the way," I explained. "She needs us to believe in her. She needs you to believe it's possible."

"I know. It's so hard to see her struggle."

We spoke a few more moments, and he had to pull himself together to get to a meeting at work. I told him I loved him, and we hung up. Then I prayed for him.

God, give him your strength to be the dad Grace Anna needs to achieve things others think she can't. Help him find the right words and the courage to be her champion and encourager.

Later that evening, he returned home with a renewed fire to give everything he had to help her learn how to walk. He continues each day to put our children before himself and to find ways to uplift them and encourage them to be their best.

One attribute he instilled in her was not to live in fear. Many times during therapies, she would face a challenge that would take deep courage to overcome.

During her first hydrotherapy session, she was terrified of the water. At three years old she had never been in water except for a bathtub. At times I felt the need to cradle her instead of forcing her to face her fear.

As I held Grace Anna, Jeff stood in front of us, motioning for her to extend her arms. She would not budge.

"Grace Anna," he chimed, "are you afraid?"

"Yes, Daddy."

"Why? You are a brave warrior. This is a big bathtub you can kick and play in," he explained. "Don't let fear keep you from having fun. Let go of Momma and move your arms like me." He made a butterfly motion in the water.

It wasn't what he said but his confidence. She knew he would take care of her if something happened. So, she dove, dove with every ounce of power in her body out into the water to swim.

She couldn't quite do it on her own, but she wasn't afraid thanks to Jeff's encouragement.

Jeff has always been handy around the house, but his skills really helped in developing or adapting Grace Anna's therapy equipment.

He built her first set of parallel bars out of PVC pipe and some creativity. In no time, he had it finished. The bars were similar to what would be found on a staircase except they went straight across the floor instead of going up or down. Grace Anna could use the bars to balance herself as she learned to walk. Since Grace Anna grows bilaterally, the right side had to be built higher than the left side due to her left-side limbs being longer than her right-side limbs. It was amazing to me how well he built them in such a short amount of time.

"Wow, Dad, these are cool," she said as she took her first stride.

"Do you like them?"

"I love them. Watch me walk."

In no time, Grace Anna coasted across the floor using the parallel bars. This amazing piece of equipment helped her learn how to walk. It also helped Jeff realize he played just as an important part in her becoming independent as I did.

We tried to come up with more fun ways to help strengthen her legs. It is hard at times to keep children motivated to continue physical therapy. We thought of a pool, but it was more of an investment than we had the money for at the time.

We continued to brainstorm until we came up with the idea of a tricycle. Bicycles and tricycles are wonderful for building strength in the legs, but how would we find one for Grace Anna that would accommodate her disproportional frame?

We looked online for weeks, losing valuable time during which we could have been getting her stronger. We found some systems, but most of them were too large for Grace Anna or the price was completely unaffordable for us.

I was at Walmart and came upon a tricycle made by Radio Flyer. I brought it home, but her legs couldn't reach the peddles. I was so frustrated.

Jeff arrived from work and immediately began modifying the tricycle to work for Grace Anna. He tried foam shoe inserts and lifts. Nothing was working. Then he went to our shed and found some old wood blocks that were left over from when we remodeled our home.

He measured, trimmed, and sanded them until Grace Anna could place her feet on the blocks to push.

The next issue was to get her feet to stay on.

I had always heard you can use duct tape to do about anything, and that is exactly what he used. He placed a pair of her shoes on the blocks and duct taped them on. He left enough room to slide Grace Anna's feet in, then he tightened the shoes.

The first few days, she struggled to push at all. He never became discouraged.

He would run around in front of us acting silly, encouraging her to get him. He made a game out of therapy. He would give her a small push from behind, and she would scream in excitement.

Within three weeks, Grace Anna could start peddling on her own and make rounds around the inside of our home. It was so thrilling to see her enjoying something that helped her become stronger.

Jeff had once again used his natural skills to make a big difference in Grace Anna's life. The doubts he felt about being good with kids were outdated.

Each day he learned more things he could do to provide Grace Anna opportunities for success, but he also taught her it was all right to fail sometimes.

Learning to catch a ball was not simple for Grace Anna. Between the thickness of her glasses and problems with depth perception, she struggled to catch a ball. Jeff would sit on the floor like a kid himself, dropping the ball on purpose sometimes to help her realize everyone messes up.

At first, she was furious and wanted to give up. Jeff was not having it.

"You can do this. If it drops, just try again. You are going to get this."

As usual with Grace Anna, her anger quickly turned into laughter. Between him diving for balls to them bouncing off his head, she was more determined than ever to master catching a ball. After a few weeks, sure enough she could catch the ball and nail him in the head when throwing it back. Thank goodness it was a soft ball.

Their bond continued to grow each day, and the abundance of love between them grew. The quiet, strong man I had married now exhibited a huge, tender heart and showed a much softer side than he had early in our relationship.

Over time his doubts disappeared, and his feelings of loss healed. God had taken hurdles in Grace Anna's walk to show Jeff he was able to reveal every part of himself to his family and not fear disappointing us.

The birth of a child alters the adults we are and can influence us to become even greater than we could ever imagine. I believe God placed Grace Anna in Jeff's life not only for Jeff to take good care of her, but because Jeff needed Grace Anna to initiate a metamorphosis from his reserved, inwardly focused self to a more confident person, concerned for others before himself.

Grace Anna would need her daddy to be strong but also tender in the days to come, to help her face challenges little girls don't normally face.

10

OH, SAY CAN YOU SEE

It's funny how when you're busy living what you consider routine days, one day can turn into something spectacular. Grace Anna had made it through a major spine surgery, cast changes, eye surgeries, and all kinds of procedures and therapies. Our family had started to show signs of adapting to the introduction of our fabulous girl to our lives.

Grace Anna continued to sing very well. She was singing songs most three-year-old little girls don't exactly think about learning, like bluegrass favorites from when I was a child, gospel hymns, and patriotic songs.

Our family is very proud of our country and the freedoms it provides for its citizens. We also had many ancestors who served in our military throughout history. My grandpa Virtreas served in the army during World War II, while my grandpa Vernon served in the army during the Korean War. Jeff's great-grandpa George had fought in the Civil War for the Union Army, his grandpa Henry served in the army during World War I, and his dad, Wyatt, served in the army during World War II, even being an honor guard at General Patton's funeral. We are very passionate about honoring our veterans and our country.

We took pride in teaching our children songs that represent the love we have for our country and the respect we feel for the men and women who have provided us with our precious freedom.

Grace Anna loved singing "America the Beautiful," "My Country 'Tis of Thee," and "God Bless the USA," but her favorite by far was "The Star-Spangled Banner." Our national anthem is very dear to my heart also. Most times I teared up hearing it. Grace Anna loved the dynamics of the song, and she seemed to absorb every note when she sang it.

One evening after her daily bath, she and I were dressing her on our living room couch. As usual we both were singing everything from "Amazing Grace" to "Stuck Like Glue" by Sugarland. She and I both enjoyed all genres of music if there wasn't any vulgarity.

"Do you want to sing the anthem?" I asked Grace Anna.

"Yeah!"

My cell phone happened to be on the coffee table. I decided to video it, thinking some of my far-off friends and family would enjoy it. She had most of the words down, but still hadn't mastered it completely, so I started it off with her.

The words flowed from her little body with great boldness and joy, and with such intensity she literally shook. The excitement built for the big finish, which she absolutely loved to belt out.

"And the home of the braaaaaaaaave!" she sang at the top of her lungs.

I stopped my camera on my phone. "Peanut, that was wonderful."

She grinned from ear to ear. She was so very proud of herself. Music was life to Grace Anna. She lit up when she sang, and from a very young age, it seemed she knew exactly the passion and emotion to add to the song to make it effective.

We continued to sing a while, then we started on her physical therapy. Getting her muscles warm in the bath always made therapy a little more tolerable for her. She gave her best during therapy. Each day it amazed me how she thrived during the many types of exercises we would do. We would make a game of therapy, always including fun, creative ways to keep her motivated.

I decided to post the video to the Facebook and YouTube pages I had created to connect with families we had met throughout our hospital visits. Social media was also an easy way to allow our family, spread out across the country, to see how she was doing.

They will love this, I thought as I uploaded the video to YouTube.

We went to bed, and I never really thought much more about the video. Grace Anna had sung so many songs to us it was commonplace to hear her sing like this. Our main hope was that those families we had gotten so close to during hospital stays enjoyed it.

After a long day of cleaning, grading papers, and doing what moms do, I lay down for some much-needed sleep. In the middle of the night, the phone rang.

"Hello?"

"Am I speaking with Angela Rodgers?" the lady asked.

"Yes, this is she. Who is this? You do know it's midnight?"

"I am so sorry it's so late, but we wanted you to know we loved your daughter's video. Sammy played it at one of his concerts today. He even told the crowd this little girl is what America is all about," she explained.

"Who is this?"

"Oh goodness, I represent Sammy Kershaw. He loved Grace Anna's video," she said, laughing. "I should have told you that from the start."

"Thank you so much. We hope everyone enjoyed it."

She had found my home phone number on my Facebook personal account. Looking back, listing my phone number there probably wasn't a great idea, but she was extremely kind and supportive.

I wondered if anyone else had watched it, so I rolled out of bed and checked.

I was in shock.

"Jeff, Jeff, Jeff!" I yelled. "Wake up!"

"What is it?"

"Sammy Kershaw's rep just called us, and Grace Anna's video has gone viral."

"Viral?"

"Yes, look!" I gave him a look of crazy shock.

Her video had over 200,000 views on YouTube, and her Facebook page had exploded with followers. We both sat in chairs at the computer, looking through pages and pages of comments and well wishes. It was unbelievable to us that so many people had started following her within a week.

We kept looking at each other, in awe of how Grace Anna's rendition of the national anthem had spread throughout the United States. It was astounding.

"Oh my goodness, she is amazing!" one post read.

"America has a new sweetheart. I can't believe a girl that young can sing that well. Way to go Grace Anna!" another read.

"This makes me proud to be an American again," someone added.

The positive posts continued for pages. It felt as if the world saw what we had already seen in Grace Anna—pure love. Tears ran down my face as Jeff and I hugged each other. We had faced so much since we had married. This was a moment we would never forget: Our baby girl had showed them. Our little miracle we had prayed for was letting the world know she was here.

Well, that was the end of my sleeping for the night. I lay awake wondering what this meant for our family. I've seen people catapult to fame and burn out like a Roman candle. Part of me was excited her video garnered so much attention, but part of me was also terrified of what could come from so many people viewing it.

Grace Anna had disabilities, and I knew that some people could be harsh and mean if you didn't look like what people considered "normal." She was perfect to us, but in our society a certain percentage were liable to pick her apart, as well as us.

The next day I couldn't get my mind off it. As I rocked Grace Anna, I kept looking at her, almost laughing inside at how she had no idea how many people were watching her all over the world. She was happy eating her cookies and watching *Peppa Pig*. The phone rang, and my brother-in-law had to add his two cents.

"I told you so," Jamie said. "I knew when you put it up, something was going to happen. It's a special video."

"I thought it was sweet, but I had no idea people would react this way."

Soon our phones rang off the hook. Our inbox flooded with emails from people wanting to know more about Grace Anna. Even though it was a great honor for people to respond to the video, it became overwhelming.

I felt the need to answer every email and every message. Jeff on the other hand thought I was focusing too much on it.

"Let some of the emails go," he said. "You don't have to answer every one of them."

I knew he was right, but the people pleaser in me felt like I would hurt their feelings if I did not reply. Between teaching full time, taking care of Grace Anna, and trying to manage the interactions related to her video, my responsibilities were getting the best of me.

I wasn't sleeping, I stayed tired, and I had no time to do anything to relax. It was taking a toll on my body and time away from my family and faith. I had to do a reality check.

"I'm not Superwoman, try as I might," I told Jeff. "I'm going to back off a little from reading everything."

"Good," he replied. "Now you go back to concentrating on yourself a little."

I cut my time down to an hour a week to go through messages and prioritize those I thought needed a quick response. It was very easy to get caught up in the firestorm of fame. Reading how wonderful your child is has an intense draw, but her fans didn't know how hard Grace Anna had it.

While her popularity came, Grace Anna still struggled with her health. After doctors removed her body cast, she developed a bursa on the back of her spine. A bursa is a fluid-filled sac that usually develops over joints. This one had formed above a screw in Grace Anna's spinal hardware, and her predicament weighed on our minds daily.

We had to watch very carefully every time we picked her up or moved her, and the bursa made her extremely uncomfortable. Doctors also had to adapt her back brace to include a protective hump to keep the bursa from bursting open. We were hoping it wouldn't. If it did, she would have to go into surgery again.

With the popularity of Grace Anna's video, our simple life had turned upside down, but her health concerned us more than anything. With all the love shown throughout the country, it was hard at times to remain steady in a whirlwind of newfound fame. Our lives would be under a microscope from then on, and Grace Anna would be known as the little girl who sang "The Star-Spangled-Banner."

God answered our prayers, allowing us to be Grace Anna's parents, so we wanted to provide her with the best life possible. We also felt the need to protect her from anything that could cause her harm. Fear of the unknown crept in, trying to stop us from following paths that seemed too rugged to try. Our faith was very important in the future decisions we would make.

That one video of the two of us being daughter and momma had struck a chord with the world. In the days to come, we would be even more astounded by the amount of love and inspiration Grace Anna provided others. We would trust God to navigate the road ahead. Big changes waited on the horizon.

SMALL-TOWN HERO TO INTERNET SENSATION

Unexpected events in life often shape the people we become. How we react to those events can help others. Grace Anna's video gave our family the opportunity to bring awareness—not only to how amazing she was, but to her genetic disorder and the lives of children with severe health issues.

Our small town had supported us spiritually, praying for us each step of the way. At one time in our local newspaper's church news, Grace Anna's name was on every list. We were so thankful we lived in an area where people believed in prayer and the power of God's mercy and grace.

Larry Rowell, the local newspaper editor, even did a feature article on Grace Anna, highlighting her many health struggles and talents. He pointed out something that had become obvious to Jeff and me: "Thanks to the Internet, all the world has become a stage for one little girl who has captured the hearts of people around the globe with her singing ability."

Our small county had a population of roughly sixteen thousand, and Grace Anna was quite popular everywhere we went. People showered her with compliments and small gifts, spoiling our dumpling. She couldn't get enough of it. She loved the interaction with people; it was if she was born to be an entertainer.

With all her health problems, you would never know Grace Anna wrestled with pain. When she was around people, the energy between them seemed to alleviate her pain. She fed off their joy.

Grace Anna's story pulled our community together with love. They treated her with adoration and warmth. I saw people I never dreamed of being compassionate melt like butter when Grace Anna was around them. Her ability to share God's light inspired me to look at our hometown differently.

I had always thought it was a little town with nothing to offer, but I was proven wrong. Our town brimmed with the most important thing it could have: amazing people. People who went to the ends of the earth to help our little girl and our family. I felt so blessed to be a part of our community.

Once outside of our hometown, life as we knew it was over. Grace Anna's doctors' visits and trips turned into meet and greets once people realized who she was. It was very sweet most of the time, but at times it scared me a little.

"Oh my gosh," a woman screamed as she bolted across the mall, heading straight for us.

I stared at her. "Are you okay?"

"It's her! Grace Anna!" she yelled, jumping up and down gasping for air.

I figured within a few moments I would be picking her up from fainting. My mom scooted over to stand at Grace's feet, creating a barrier between them. We didn't know if she was going to explode or try to grab her. Everyone in the mall stared at us, and I didn't know what to do.

"Can I help you?" I asked.

"I love your daughter. I love her. She's amazing. Oh please, please, can I say hello to her?"

"Okay, let's take some deep breaths and calm down. I think you will scare her if you don't calm down," I tried explaining to the lady.

She took some deep breaths and slowly returned to what I

consider normal behavior. I wasn't trying to be mean, but it was freaking me out. The momma grizzly bear inside me kicked into protection mode. "You can say hi to her, but wer're on our way out, so we can't stay long."

She knelt and reached out to touch Grace Anna's knee, which caused my mom to scoot even closer to Grace Anna. "Grace Anna, I love you," the lady said softly. "You make my day so much better. Keep singing, sweetie. I'll be watching."

Once she finished, she stood up, hugged me, then walked away. I think she realized she had startled us. She more than likely was a wonderful woman, but I had never seen someone act so bizarre for Grace Anna. It was sinking in that our lives were not private anymore. People knew Grace Anna and loved her; she had become a sensation. We needed to prepare ourselves for changes.

Our days of doctors' visits now were greeted with fans of Grace Anna's page and people proclaiming their joy from watching Grace Anna's video. My doctor's appointment was no exception.

It was time for my yearly exam, and I was looking forward to it. Sounds kind of crazy, but every time I went to my yearly exam, I could allow Grace Anna to minister to a doctor that suggested we abort her. My dad traveled with me in case I needed someone to help with Grace Anna.

The doctor had not given us much hope when I was pregnant, and when he suggested an abortion, it broke my heart. I had always loved him as a doctor. He delivered Isaiah, and I trusted him completely when it came to delivering babies. I was shocked he offered abortions. I would have never guessed it.

After my exam, I had my usual conversation about Grace Anna. "How is she doing?" he asked.

"Really well. I guess you've heard about her big song," I replied, hoping he had.

"Yes, I have."

Grace Anna chimed in. "I can sing. I am a good singer."

He grinned at her. I could tell he was enthralled by her. I

wondered if he thought about what he suggested I do when I was pregnant. Did he regret saying it? Did it even cross his mind?

As he walked me to the nurse's station to check out, one of the nurses complimented her singing. Then before I knew it, Grace Anna belted out one of her signature songs.

"Amazing grace, how sweet the sound."

The staff stood up from their desks and moved to a tight circle around her. It was if her singing hypnotized them. No other sound was heard in the office. Thirty or more people stood listening to her give her testimony, including the doctor that wanted to abort her.

Tears streaming down the people's faces showered my spirit. "Oh God, I know this is you. Thank you," I whispered.

Once she finished, an eruption of clapping overtook the office, and my dad came running to the door. He knew what it was. He knew once again her innocent spirit had captured peoples' hearts. I hoped in my spirit it touched my doctor. I couldn't see how it wouldn't.

Now hopefully when he spoke to a woman with a less than ideal pregnancy, Grace Anna would enter his mind and he would think twice about offering an abortion. Maybe he would see that every life has a divine purpose and deserves a chance.

As we made our way to the exit, I looked at my doctor and smiled. I wanted to tell him to wake up, but I realized God already showed him.

After that visit, I understood the impact of her story. I saw first-hand how people reacted to her in a big way. The charisma she embodied had the power to change the hearts and minds of people.

Sometimes people would ask about Grace Anna's condition right in front of her. "What's wrong with her? Why does she wear thick glasses? Why isn't she walking?"

When we heard questions like these, it was hard to interact with people. At first, I was nice and walked them through her condition, but I didn't want Grace Anna being defined by her disorder. She was a girl like all other girls. I didn't want her to always be labeled as "the little girl with Conradi."

I began replying, "Nothing's wrong with her. She does have a genetic condition called Conradi-Hünermann. She's very smart, beautiful, and so talented."

For some reason, after that they tended to focus on Grace Anna as a person instead of a disorder. I wrote articles for online sites educating others on Conradi, and I also explained her condition on her Facebook page. The more I educated people, the less they tended to bring it up.

I didn't mind educating people about her disorder. I just didn't want that to be the only thing they discussed around her. I never wanted her to feel less of a person because of a disorder or that God had not made her perfectly in His image. She was a miracle, and God never made a child wrong.

With all of that educating, I was confident I knew when someone was insulting my daughter. As usual, when I became a little too confident, God showed me I still needed to give compassion and understanding to others.

In life, we sometimes view television personalities as distant people who lack the same feelings as the people we see every day. It's very easy at times to think news anchors are robotic humans without the same struggles we have. A comment by a news anchor would lead to an opportunity for me to realize that fame does not turn people into uncaring people.

As I was reading through the messages on Grace Anna's Facebook page, one in particular stood out to me, mainly because the writer had written in all caps, and the name of a cartoon character, Mr. Magoo, was at the very beginning.

"Oh my goodness, Ms. Rodgers, she called your daughter Mr. Magoo," the message explained.

What was this person talking about? Mr. Magoo? How could someone think that about my daughter? She's beautiful. I grew angrier by the minute.

I was furious not only because of what was said but because it was said on national television for the entire world to see. I searched and searched for the clip of Kyra Phillips comparing my daughter to Mr. Magoo. It was evident she had said it. CNN's Facebook page, along with Grace Anna's, had gobs of posts about it. But for the life of me, I couldn't find it.

When I received the message, I was on my way to a sleep study. I knew I couldn't sleep if I didn't say something to somebody about the clip, so what did I do? I called CNN.

Thankfully no one answered. If they had, more than likely my temper would have brought out the worst in me, but they did have an answering machine. Ah, those things don't let you erase.

"Hello, my name is Angela Rodgers. My daughter is Grace Anna Rodgers that you featured on one of your shows today. I was beyond disappointed that Kyra Phillips compared my daughter to Mr. Magoo. It's shameful that a news anchor could make fun of a little girl with disabilities. How is that allowed on your network? Please return my call as soon as you can. I would love to speak to someone about this."

I left my number and figured I would never hear back from them.

I woke from my sleep study and drove home. As I entered the house, the phone was ringing. *It's 7:00 a.m. Who in the world could be calling?*

"Hello?"

"Hi, I'm trying to reach Angela Rodgers," a woman said.

"This is she."

"This is Kyra Phillips. I would like to speak to you about my broadcast yesterday."

She barely got out the sentence before breaking down into sorrowful sobbing. I felt horrible. When she tried to get another word out, she began crying again. I didn't know what to do, so I waited for her to gather her thoughts.

"Ms. Rodgers, I am so sorry. Mr. Magoo holds a special place in my heart. My grandpa used to tell me I was as cute as Mr. Magoo. It was not meant to be disrespectful in any way. I have a sister with Down syndrome. I work to help better the lives of children with disabilities. I feel horrible. I would never do anything to insult Grace Anna. She is precious."

Then I felt horrible and began to sob. "I didn't see the clip. I trusted the word of her page followers. Now that you've explained it, I can see your intentions weren't vicious." I barely kept my composure.

"I can see how they thought that, not knowing my story, but I sincerely want to apologize for anything that may have hurt you, Grace Anna, and your family. I truly am sorry from the depths of my soul."

I believed her. She didn't have to call me. She could of have asked one of her assistants to call. It was eye-opening to understand that how we see each other reflects our life experiences. Mr. Magoo was a childhood treasure to her, where to me he was an ugly old cartoon character. I had to forgive her. I didn't believe her intentions were to hurt us.

Kyra and I discussed how her sister had changed her life for the better and how Grace Anna had done the same for me. She was very passionate about her work with Down syndrome organizations.

As our discussion neared its end, Kyra wanted to help us find a way to complete a wheelchair-accessible bathroom for Grace Anna. She referred us to the Arc of Kentucky for help getting a grant for the bathroom.

Although the grant was awarded years later, the interaction with Kyra taught me a valuable lesson. I couldn't rush to judgment about people, no matter what they did for a living or where they came from. I also had to watch and read things said about Grace Anna and not take the word of her followers. They may have the best intentions, but misunderstandings happen.

Kyra and I still email each other a couple of times a year, checking in. I respected her greatly for calling me that day. Most people in her position would have ignored me and moved on. It took courage to call me.

I made up my mind to build my daughter's self-worth through

our family. She would know she was important, and she would be taught how to handle situations that I had been handling for her due to her age. One day she would have to stand up for herself and face difficult situations with people.

"Grace Anna, God sent you to us with a big purpose. You are just like everyone else. He has a plan for you, and there is absolutely nothing wrong with you," I told her.

"Momma, I know. I'm the best." She smiled, her dimples as huge as ever.

"You're beautiful, smart, and you are going to change the world."

She laid her head on my chest and snuggled in tightly for a hug. I continued to tell her that as often as I felt I should, reinforcing that she was fine just like she was.

I also took the opportunity on television interviews and radio interviews to educate others about Conradi and encourage listeners to focus on the child, not the disability. Grace Anna and I even created a YouTube video about her form of dwarfism to help people understand the condition.

Educating the public in the right way was important to me. I wanted people to see that not only was Grace Anna an amazing singer—she was a fighter, and they could be too. Her singing was awesome, but her story was much more important.

Educating others and sharing her story also brought us in contact with other Conradi patients. When we first started out, Grace Anna knew two children with Conradi. Then it grew to over thirty, large for such a rare disorder. Grace Anna's popularity not only brought joy to others—it helped her connect with people who shared the same struggles. Once again, she brought people together who, under normal circumstances, never would have met.

Within a month after I posted the video of Grace Anna singing the national anthem, it had been shared over ten million times. It took me quite a bit of time to wrap my mind around that fact. By the beginning of the year, her Facebook page had broken the 500,000-follower mark and another video I posted was successful too.

Her YouTube page also picked up quite a few followers and videos were being shared all over the world. Her message of hope, love, and courage touched lives we never dreamed of. Life was an exciting adventure, and Grace Anna's health was comfortably uneventful. We had finally found a balance between her popularity and enjoying being a family.

Our community continued to be a lifeline for us, especially our home church. They believed in the power of prayer and stood by us through every step we took. The support was one reason we could hold it together. When we join in one mind and one purpose, things happen.

Adjusting to Grace Anna's fame was not easy, but her story was changing the world in an encouraging way. Love spread and God's light shone through her spirit. We thought we had seen the biggest moments of Grace Anna's appeal, but what came next made our little family a household name. Grace Anna had the opportunity to tell one of the biggest country music legends ever to stop singing. Life was getting ready to be very interesting.

12

┼ER BIG DEBUT

O ur family had been interviewed on many local television and radio programs as well as some statewide stations. We thought Grace Anna's popularity had reached its peak, but we found out we were wrong. Our family was getting ready to embark onto national television, and Grace Anna was determined to make her mark.

"Hello, Angela, we would love to speak to you about appearing with Grace Anna and your family on *Katie* with Katie Couric," the email read.

Stunned, I sat at my computer, reading it over and over, making sure I wasn't hallucinating. I picked up my cell phone and dialed Jeff's number.

"Are you sitting down?" I asked.

"Why? Do I need to be?"

"I think so. We've been invited to be on Katie Couric's show."

Nothing but silence came across the line.

I waited and waited. Had he passed out? I didn't know, but I was starting to wonder. "Jeff!" I yelled. "What are you doing?"

He would never admit it, but once he returned to the line, I knew he had been crying. I could hear it in his voice. "I'm here." His voice cracked.

"Are we going to do it?"

"When?"

"I don't know. I've not called them yet."

"Find out when, and we will do it."

I called the number left in the email. Once I reached the scheduler, we set up the day for us to appear. We didn't have much time to prepare, because it was six days away.

"We can't wait to meet your family. We also have a big surprise for you."

"Thank you so much. We are excited to attend."

I wanted to go, but I was a little concerned about how quickly it was happening. I didn't want us to be unprepared for what was to come. I tried to think of someone who had been on one of these shows to give us some pointers, but I didn't know anyone. Jeff assured me that our family could appear on a show and show the world what an amazing daughter we had.

While Jeff was excited to be going, Isaiah was not. "Mom, what if I pass out? What if I stutter?" he said.

"You are not going to stutter," Jeff encouraged. "You will be fine. Just think of it as if we are all sitting on a couch at home."

We were going to be ourselves, and if America loved us, that was great, and if they didn't, that was fine too.

Once we landed at JFK International Airport, we hopped in a car the show had sent to pick us up. The driver gave us a guided tour of the city. Things up close look so different than on television. Times Square and Central Park appeared very different in person. They were breathtaking.

"Momma, look. It's so pretty," Grace Anna said, smiling as we stood at door of The Empire Hotel and the Lincoln Center for the Performing Arts. The sparkling lights captivated her.

The entire experience was magical. We would never forget seeing the skyscrapers, hearing the commotion from the streets, feeling the electricity of the city. The following day would prove to be no different. The show would be an experience we would never forget for different reasons.

"Let's go, little star," I whispered in Grace Anna's ear as I woke her up that morning. "It's time for your big debut, baby girl."

Grace Anna rolled over and sweetly smiled. I don't think she knew what the day was about, except that it was about her. I don't think she grasped how many people would be watching.

"Momma, I'm hungry," Grace Anna said. "I want pancakes."

After a delicious breakfast at the hotel, we started to get dressed. Nerves were getting to Isaiah and me, but to Jeff it seemed like just another day at the office.

He tried to calm us. "Be yourself. It will be fine."

It didn't work.

I'd imagined we would go through a walkthrough or at least meet Katie Couric before we taped the live show, but we never had the opportunity. I am a planner, so I felt a little nervous not knowing what to expect. I hoped it would all go well.

The phone rang, and the limo arrived to pick us up. We were on our way to appear on national television to tell Grace Anna's story.

Once we arrived, Katie's assistant, Jessica, greeted us. Jessica and I had been relaying emails since the previous week, sharing information and pictures for the broadcast. She led us to get our hair and makeup touched up. It was hilarious watching Isaiah and Jeff get dolled up, especially when they touched up Jeff's bald head.

"Momma, Daddy's getting makeup on." Grace Anna giggled.

"I know. They have to put extra on Daddy's head because it shines so bright."

Jeff laughed along with us, but Isaiah was so nervous he couldn't find much humor in anything.

"Mom, what if I pass out?" He wrung his hands. "I don't know if I can do this."

"Here is an outline of the things Katie might ask. You can look those over, and that way you won't be so surprised if she asks you something," Jessica explained.

I was very thankful for that list! Not just for Isaiah but for me. It helped me relax a little myself, but I wouldn't tell Isaiah I was nervous. He needed me to be the calm, pulled-together mom at this moment.

Jessica escorted us to the greenroom before going onstage. We could watch the show going on, but for some reason, it cut off after a few moments. *That's funny*, I thought. *Why would they not want us to see the show?*

Grace Anna played and laughed as she always did. Nothing ever seemed to bother her much. Jeff, Isaiah, and I talked with the staff and sipped some drinks they had provided.

"Okay, guys, they are ready for you," Jessica said. "Let's go."

As we headed up the walkway, the crew greeted us. It was amazing to see the network of people that put the show together—more than I would have expected. I wished I had told someone about Grace Anna's fear of loud noises, but Jeff and I forgot. It sure would have helped settle things down the first few minutes of our time on the show.

"And here she is. Grace Anna, her mom, Angie, dad, Jeff, and her brother, Isaiah," Katie said as she introduced us onto her show.

As we walked across the stage, the lights shone extremely brightly and the crowd clapped very loudly. I knew more than likely what would happen next and it did. Grace Anna started crying.

Ever since her ear tubes were put in, she had issues with loud noises. The clapping startled her so much she wouldn't turn to face the crowd for a few moments. *Oh no*, I thought. *I hope to goodness she settles down in a few moments.*

Once we sat down, Katie tried to calm Grace Anna. She even offered to hold her, but Grace Anna wouldn't have any of that. She wanted her momma, and she didn't want to be there. I felt so horrible for her.

As I tried to reassure her everything was okay, Katie introduced Grace Anna's video of singing the national anthem. Maybe it was seeing herself on such a big screen, but it calmed her a little. She was fine if she didn't leave my arms. As they say in show business: the show must go on.

Katie asked me, "Could you describe how the video happened?"

I described the day as it occurred, but I started feeling very hot. My heart raced and my chest felt as if it would burst open. I was having a panic attack. I'd had panic attacks before. They could be horrible. I remembered the techniques I learned to help them: breathe through my nose and out through my mouth, then focus on the words "I will be fine." I had to let my body realize I was fine.

I can barely remember anything I said, then Katie turned to Jeff. "Jeff, can you tell us about Grace Anna's condition?"

Jeff sounded like a doctor as he described Conradi-Hünermann syndrome perfectly. "There are many things that go along with her type of dwarfism. Besides short stature, she deals with extremely dry skin, cataracts, misshapen bones, and some hearing problems."

He seemed so calm and collected. It shocked me. I felt incredibly proud of the way he gave everyone a glimpse of Grace Anna's life.

Katie then turned to Isaiah. "How do you feel about your little sister?"

"I'm proud of her, and I love her," Isaiah nervously blurted out. Bless his heart. He was terrified being on the stage in front of everyone.

As I listened to Katie describe how she loved Grace Anna, I wondered if she knew I was thinking, *I can't believe I'm this close to Katie Couric.* She was like anyone else—very sweet, kind, and beautiful.

"Grace Anna, we have someone here that thinks you're pretty wonderful too. Come on out, woman." Katie turned to a surprise guest rounding the corner.

It was Naomi Judd, and she was carrying a big basket of toys for Grace Anna.

As Naomi sat down between Jeff and me, she started singing to Grace Anna, "Amazing grace, how sweet the sound."

Then it happened.

"Stop singing my song," Grace Anna scolded. "That's *my* song."

"Oh, I'm so sorry," Naomi said, then she sang, "You're a brick house."

Grace Anna didn't like that one either, but she did love the toys Naomi brought, especially all the Sesame Street characters. She grabbed Elmo and gave him a big hug.

"I think you are a superstar, sweetheart." Naomi patted Grace Anna's hand.

I wanted to break down in tears, to run over and hug Naomi Judd, but afraid of seeming like an overdramatic crazy woman, I quietly said, "Thank you so much, Miss Judd."

I had watched Naomi Judd many times growing up. I sang right along with her, and she had just told my daughter she was a superstar. My mind was blown. I didn't know how God had done this, but I was very grateful our family had the opportunity.

Our segment of the show wrapped up with a montage of pictures of Grace Anna as we got up to leave the stage. Katie and Naomi joined us to snap a photo of the experience. Both ladies as well as the staff were absolutely wonderful to us.

Once off the set, we erupted in laughter. Our little ol' family from rural Kentucky was on national television. Our sweet girl had made her national television debut, and boy, was it an experience—maybe not as we had planned, but it was something we would always remember and cherish.

As we returned to the airport to go home, I tried to jot down the events in my journal. I wanted to capture the joy we had once again experienced by Grace Anna being Grace Anna. I also pondered how sweet it was to see Isaiah so nervous to tell the world how proud he was of his sister. The experience drew our family closer, and we felt happier than we had in a long time.

It was a once-in-a-lifetime experience for us all.

Not only was Grace Anna's story displayed for the world—we educated people about her disorder. Plus, we met a country music legend from our own state.

At the same time, Grace Anna made it clear she was a little girl who only wanted to be a little girl. Our choices greatly affected her. Even though she was never in danger, the show upset her because we forgot to communicate her aversion to loud sounds. We decided as a family that until she was quite a bit older, she would not do a program unless we were able to get her accustomed to the surroundings. Also, if she didn't want to do it, we wouldn't.

Sometimes, in the middle of struggles, God sends incredible joyous experiences—experiences we learn and grow from. Our time at the *Katie* show brought a little girl's story that would not normally be heard to America's front view. It helped our family meet wonderful people doing great things to help the world.

God once again used a little girl who was given no hope to give others hope through simply being her sweet little self. That experience would also bring more amazing people into our lives—people who would help Grace Anna live her life more easily every day. We would gain a host of incredible people from all over the world that would become our extended family.

We had no idea that our tiny little gal would one day inspire millions of people.

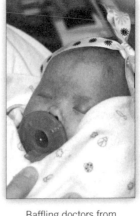

Baffling doctors from the beginning.

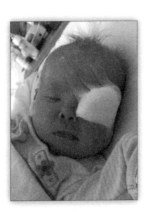

Her first eye surgery at a little over two months old.

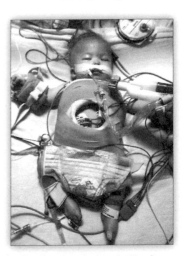

The first day of a long battle after Grace Anna's first spine surgery.

One of Grace Anna's favorite things to do is fish at the family pond with Daddy.

Grace Anna can always find joy,
even when she's heading for surgery.

Taking a break from homeschool to chow down
on a peanut butter and jelly sandwich.

Paying respect to Pa Virtreas,
one of the many veterans in our family.

Grace Anna wholeheartedly
believes that God will answer
her prayers.

Grace Anna definitely loves the University of Kentucky Wildcats, just like her Bubba.

We rescued Oscar as a small kitten, and he has brought immense joy to Grace Anna.

Her favorite animal is the cat, so she will not part with any toy cat her fans and family have given her.

At her keyboard station doing what she loves best— singing and playing music.

We've always instilled in Grace Anna that she is beautiful and that this shines from within.

13

THE KINDNESS OF STRANGERS

The growth of Grace Anna's popularity not only brought light to Conradi-Hünermann syndrome; it brought a giant base of people who connected to her in a profound way. I set aside specific hours each week to comb through the letters, emails, and messages. I realized almost every one of them mentioned two things: hope and inspiration.

One of my first correspondences was from a lady with an adult son with cerebral palsy. She sent me a link to a video of her wheelchair-bound son singing "You Are My Sunshine" along with Grace Anna's video. He was clapping and singing at the top of his lungs with a huge smile. I must have watched the video a hundred times, each time shedding more tears.

The level of joy he felt singing with Grace Anna struck me. It was as if his spirit directly connected to Grace Anna's. They had a similar glow about them, as if it was more than singing but a moment of pure, innocent wonder.

I sent a quick email back to his mom: "Joy and love poured from your video. It touched not only my heart but my entire family. We are honored he sang with Grace Anna. She herself watched the video with me many, many times, singing right along with him. We will be praying for you and look forward to hearing from you again."

Those moments are the ones that touched our hearts deeply—people living very similar lives to ours. They knew what we were going through, and they could share the knowledge of what was truly important in life. Making his life the tiniest bit better meant the world to us, and it all happened by Grace Anna being her sweet self.

The letters and emails continued to pour in; many of them included money. I didn't like dealing with monetary gifts connected to Grace Anna, but loads of people continued to insist that they help her in some way. Jeff and I discussed our options. He, like me, wanted to do the right thing in a positive manner.

"What if you set up an account to actually help Grace Anna?" Jeff said. "And the money was used to better her life."

"I guess that would be okay, but I don't want people thinking we are begging for money."

We racked our brains trying to figure out what Grace Anna could greatly benefit from. The main thing she needed was a bedroom on the bottom floor and a wheelchair-accessible bathroom. That meant we would have to build her an all-new facility or a new living room and kitchen.

The living room and kitchen addition would mean those rooms could be turned into bedrooms and possibly a new bathroom. Plus, our current surroundings were not very conducive for a wheelchair. We opted for an open living room and kitchen that would be easy for her to move around in. We'd move her bedroom down beside one for us.

This would give Grace Anna a space she could safely get to. The price was more than we expected, however. A wheelchair-accessible bathroom is not cheap, so we tried our best to put that in there also.

We contacted the bank and learned that Grace Anna could lose her Medicaid if she received any funds. Then we considered other options. We decided to set up a GoFundMe Campaign to help with the expenses. People wanted to give, and this was the best option. Everyone could see how much money we received and what we did with it.

"Oh my goodness, Jeff," I said, running into the living room. "Look at this."

"Good grief!" he exclaimed. "How in the world did this happen?"

Enough money was donated to build Grace Anna a bedroom downstairs. We would have to wait on the wheelchair-accessible bathroom.

We quickly hired our neighbor to frame the house, and we finished the inside on our own, showing pictures as we progressed. We saved so much money doing it on our own that it helped us add features that would enhance Grace Anna's life even more.

One day as I was combing through the many emails, I noticed one from a bank. Most of the time these things were frauds, but this one looked very official. I called the number listed.

"Hello, this is Angela Rodgers. I received an email about an anonymous donation."

"Yes, ma'am, one of our customers would like to help your daughter, Grace Anna, with a donation."

Although I loved the person's compassion for Grace Anna, I wanted to know the person's name to thank them and make sure it wasn't someone wanting to invade our lives. I expressed my concerns to the bank employee and gave her my private number. I was so surprised when I received a phone call the next day.

As my cell phone rang, the name Lauren O'Reilly popped up in the caller ID. I had no idea who that was.

"Hello, Angela, my name is Lauren," the woman said. "You may have heard of my family's business, O'Reilly Auto Parts."

"Yes, ma'am, I certainly have."

"I'm a huge fan of Grace Anna's, and I felt God lead me to help her in some way."

Lauren and I talked for a long time. She felt compelled to help us, and who was I to tell her she couldn't bless Grace Anna. She told me of her family's humble startup of O'Reilly Auto Parts and how her faith was extremely important to her. Lauren had a very sweet and kind spirit. Once again, it was as if I had known her my entire life.

Lauren had given us a gift from her heart, and we had connected with each other on a spiritual level. She made a very distinct impression on my heart that day. She also, along with Grace Anna's followers, gave Grace Anna a wonderful place she could call her own and a home she could move freely in.

Once we were finished, we posted pictures of Grace Anna in her new room.

"Oh, Momma, I love it," she said.

We filled her new pink bedroom with things she loved, especially musical toys. She looked around in amazement. Everything was finished near Christmas, so we sent a Christmas card from our family to all the people who donated to the fund. It was the least we could do, considering the level of generosity we had received.

The kindness of all those people felt like a huge hug. They got us. They knew what Grace Anna had been through and wanted to be part of a solution for us. We had gained not simply Facebook followers but an enormous extended family. We were not alone in this anymore.

I continued to read messages expressing how Grace Anna had changed the lives of many people. One counselor even told us she used Grace Anna's videos to help teens considering suicide to find hope in their lives. The more messages I read, the more I knew we had made the right decision earlier to keep the page up. People were having real experiences that enriched their lives through her videos, and we never had to go anywhere to do it.

One message caught my eye as I scanned through them one late evening.

"My daughter has Conradi too. We would love to meet you," Nicole wrote.

Nicole was stationed at an army base near Grace Anna's spine doctor. She was raising her two beautiful daughters, Ava and Addie, on her own. Ava also had Conradi-Hünermann syndrome. Ava was four months older than Grace Anna and, boy, did they favor. It was uncanny how similar the girls looked.

"Maybe some time when Grace Anna has a checkup we can meet you at the hospital," she wrote.

"We would love that," I replied.

I had already looked through every picture and message on Nicole's Facebook page, checking to make sure she wasn't a possible threat to Grace Anna. What I found was one tough cookie.

There she was, experiencing every heartache with Ava's health that we had experienced with Grace Anna—every struggle, every setback—but she was doing it alone. Yet, she didn't post about feeling sorry for herself in the many challenges she faced. I was drawn to her resilience and love for her children.

When Ava turned the corner in the cafeteria at the hospital, my heart filled with overwhelming joy. Grace Anna had a confidant, someone who knew what she faced every day and could understand her life. Try as we might, we truly didn't understand her pain at times. Ava knew exactly what Grace Anna went through. Grace Anna and Ava were connected on a deep level that no one except those with Conradi could understand.

Nicole was never at a loss for words.

"Oh my goodness, they look just alike. They have the same hair, the same glasses. This is crazy. I started to believe we would never meet another person with Conradi."

I don't know if she was nervous or excited, but she burst with information for us. It was breathtaking to sit back and listen to Nicole and watch her facial expressions as she described what Ava had faced over her short life.

This must be what I'm like.

So many times, I'd wished I had someone to discuss Grace Anna with—someone who would understand my ranting about her daily battles. I knew Nicole and her daughters would become a big part of our lives.

Even more touching was Grace Anna and Ava's interactions with each other. You would have thought they were sisters. They hugged, laughed, and carried on like old pals. Several people walking by stopped to ask if they were twins. They developed quite a connection that day.

Grace Anna didn't have any buddies at home to play with on a regular basis. The newfound friendships with Ava and Addie excited her. She was in heaven.

Several hours later, when the food had grown cold and the girls were tired, we had to move on to Grace Anna's appointment. I bent down and hugged Ava's neck. "I am so glad I met you."

With a big grin, she looked in my eyes. "Me too."

It was a hugging bonanza. I don't know why we didn't do one big group hug. It would have been quicker.

That meeting began something special for both families. Not only did the children connect, the adults did too. The three of us became very close over the next few months, talking through FaceTime and emails. On our next trip to the hospital, we decided to do an extended visit and stay with them for the weekend.

Jeff doesn't like to stay at someone else's house. He cherishes his privacy, but for Grace Anna he would give it a try. He also wanted to be there for other reasons.

"I don't know how a dad could not be there when his little girl is having surgery," Jeff said. "How can Ava's dad not be there for her?"

Ava had made a big impression on Jeff. He looked at her the same way he saw Grace Anna. His paternal instincts made him feel the need to protect her. Jeff made a point to brag on Ava and tried his best to encourage her every chance he got.

We spent the weekend learning about each other, meeting their friends, and enjoying the great state of Virginia. Our time was filled with laughter, good food, and bonding.

"I'm so glad we did this," I said to Nicole. "You all are a godsend. I'm so grateful we've been brought together."

"We love you all and want you to come back anytime."

We did. Many, many times. Every time we went to Baltimore for doctors' appointments, they took us in and treated us like family. To us they already were family. We looked forward to our visits every four months. These trips were like mini vacations for us. Grace Anna got to have a sleepover with friends, something she didn't experience at home.

Sadly, though, our trips to stay with Nicole and her daughters would soon end. She was being transferred to another state. We were devastated. We loved being with them so much, and this would mean Grace Anna would lose those days of being with two little girls she adored. I refused to allow the change to break the bond that had been created.

Distance did not keep us from being friends. With today's technology, we communicated more than most friends who lived near each other, sharing moments of our lives that mattered the most to us. Nicole even drove the long way to spend days with us in Kentucky, and we made plans to make it to their new home.

The love and respect shared between our two families was incredible. Without Grace Anna and Ava having Conradi, we would have never met. We would have missed so much joy and happiness. Grace Anna and Ava had made our lives so rich, and the two of them had become lifelong sisters.

It's humorous how God brings people together—people you never dreamed you had anything in common with, people living very different lives than you do, people desperately needing someone to fill a void in their lives.

Diane was a retired CIA employee living in a small town in Illinois. She had emailed me several times, wanting to send Grace Anna some Matilda Jane outfits. I loved the outfits, but I knew they were more expensive than most things Grace Anna wore, and I didn't want to take advantage of Diane's generosity.

Diane would not take no for an answer. In a very kind way, she was very persistent with her reasons for giving Grace Anna the gifts that she felt led to give. She provided her phone number, her address, and a very extensive description of her background. She was not a stalker, she promised. I decided to let her send the outfits. She seemed very sweet, and it wasn't as if she was wanting to come to our house.

When the first package arrived, I was very impressed with the softness and quality of the outfit. Grace Anna struggles so much with things aggravating her ichthyosis. It was nice to find clothing that would be gentle on her skin. I decided to call Diane to express my gratitude.

"Hello," she answered.

"Hi, Diane, this is Grace Anna's mom."

"Oh my! I can't believe you are calling me. I adore Grace Anna."

The excitement in her voice startled me. I knew Grace Anna had a profound effect on people, but this was beyond that.

Diane did not have any siblings, and she never married. Her mother and father had passed away and the only people who remained in her life were her friends. She had been following Grace Anna since the very beginning. Diane looked at Grace Anna as if she were a granddaughter she never knew.

At first, I was a little creeped out by the conversation. How could anyone love my daughter without actually meeting her? I tried to empathize with Diane's situation, but it was hard for me to imagine being completely on my own without any family.

"I love Grace Anna," Diane continued. "She has been a light in my life. Some days her smile and joy have challenged me to get up and quit pitying myself."

"I appreciate your kindness, but I don't want you to feel like you have to shower her with gifts all the time. Your prayers and lovely letters are plenty."

I could tell she didn't like the answer, but she understood my wishes. We continued to share stories of our lives and how Grace Anna had changed our lives. She was a pleasure to talk with. I thought that would be the last time I talked to her, but it wasn't.

She persisted, emailing to check on how my day was or if Grace Anna needed anything—basically doing things a grandma would do. I don't know if she was wearing me down or if God knew she needed us in her lives and we needed her too.

Jeff knew exactly what Diane was feeling. He was an only child, and besides us, the only close family he had living was his mom and a third cousin.

"It is a scary feeling to realize you could be alone in this world one day—no family, no one that really knows you," he explained.

It was the first time I really thought about how lonely she must get at times and how hard the holidays must be on her. I saw Diane in a different light. She wasn't trying to push her way into Grace Anna's life. She was looking for someone to love.

After a year of emailing back and forth, we finally met in person at a Cracker Barrel outside of Florence, Kentucky. I figured if she was crazy, she wouldn't pull anything in a Cracker Barrel. She brought along three friends of her own. We spent two hours laughing and talking. Diane was a special lady who, in her own way, loved Grace Anna.

Her constant prayers to connect with us led to a wonderful friendship that developed over time. It started out very differently than any other friendship, but it deepened the compassion I have for people who have no family. They have a different type of struggle. She has adopted us into her heart, and we have accepted her into our little family.

The more messages I read on how Grace Anna touched people's lives, the better person I became. The very first message to the latest one all contained something in common: my daughter made their lives better. Whether someone suffered from a recent death in the family or someone recently lost their job, Grace Anna changed their lives one song at a time.

God blessed Grace Anna with a gift to sing, but He also blessed her with the ability to motivate people to keep going, to keep trying, and to believe in something better. He used her in ways I could never dream of. Our post-office box flowed with letters from all over the world, from China to Australia, from Dubai to Edinburgh—places I had never even heard of.

It was becoming evident to me that Grace Anna had a special calling on her life to change not just our family but the world. Yet, with all the wonderful people we connected to, we were getting ready to learn that where there is good, there is also evil. Grace Anna was not immune from the cruelness that exists in the world.

14

WHERE THERE IS GOOD, THERE IS BAD

Life is full of love most days. Then there are days when hate tries to break the joy that lives in your heart. God blessed us with a vast group of loving and supportive people throughout the world. I couldn't fathom that someone could dislike my daughter or wish her harm, but I would soon find out that not everyone sees hope when they look at my Grace Anna.

"Your daughter would have been better off if you had aborted her," a woman from the other side of the country wrote in a message through Grace Anna's Facebook page. "One day when other children are running and laughing out on the playground, your daughter will be sitting inside watching them from her wheelchair."

Those lines stuck out as I read the two-page message filled with criticism toward me and thoughtless conjecture about how horrible Grace Anna's life would be. An overwhelming anger filled me as I repeatedly read each line. I wanted to track this woman down, confront her, and demand an apology.

Then it dawned on me. If she feels so deeply that we've created a horrible life for Grace Anna, approaching her aggressively probably wouldn't sway her.

I clicked on her profile page and was shocked she was a married mother of two beautiful boys. She looked like someone who, if I were to run into her, would be a kind lady. How could she could look at Grace Anna so negatively?

Browsing her page, I knew I had to reply to her, but I would not allow her to steal my joy. That's the thing about life: no one can steal your joy unless you let them. I determined to make something good out of the entire process, even if it only helped me grow into a person who could rise above ignorance.

I sent her this message:

Dear Ma'am,

Although Grace Anna may seem like a burden, a problem, or maybe even a mistake to you, she most definitely is not any of those things. She was prayed for before she was ever formed in my womb, and we continue to pray for her daily. We also pray to be the parents she needs. God sent our miracle to make our lives better and to give hope to people throughout the world. I can't even start to comprehend the emptiness you must feel to make statements like you did in your message. All I can do is pray for you and tell you that Grace Anna will be loved abundantly and cared for to the best of our abilities. We will give her opportunities to live a full, happy life, and she will play on the playground with all the other kids. I hope one day you will be able to see what a blessing she is and how amazing her life is. We will be praying for you and your family. We hope you experience the joy that is possible if you just accept it. God bless you and have a great day.

I never heard back from her.

I wish I could say we've never encountered similar situations, but I can't. Later in the year, I was browsing through Grace Anna's articles online, and a website popped up dedicated to bashing our sweetheart. They had taken videos and pictures of Grace Anna without our permission to create horrible memes and videos. Some went as far as to call her a monster.

"Why would someone do this to a child?" I cried to Jeff.

"Honey, I don't know. I don't know how we can stop it either."

We both were stumped how to get a website removed. Neither one of us were very educated on the laws concerning websites. We didn't know where to start for help. Then I remembered a lady named Katrina who was part of an organization called Rise & Stand that worked to protect children from bullying. I decided to give her a call.

"Katrina, I can't believe they can do this stuff. She's a child. Aren't there any laws that protect her from being attacked like this?"

Katrina replied, "I will do some research and see what we can do. Things like this are exactly why we started our organization."

Weeks went by, and the website remained up. I became increasingly angry and determined to get the site down. I researched the topic tirelessly through search engines and websites. Still, I felt helpless. I was her momma. I was supposed to shield her from pain, and putting her in the limelight had brought people into her life who wanted to cause her harm.

In that moment, I debated removing every video, picture, and social media page we had created for Grace Anna. What if someone tried to physically attack her one day? What if they tried to hunt her down and take her from us? My mind raced through scary possibilities. I had to get out of the house, off the computer, and back to focusing on those I could help—my family.

I loaded up Grace Anna, and we went to see my grandma Mary Belle. Grandma had dementia, and her health was fading. Grandma had never been a lady who showed her emotions very well, but with Grace Anna, she melted like butter. She would crack me up, insisting Grace Anna took after her family; they were all short. I tried to explain it was dwarfism, but it was no use. To her Grace Anna was just short like her family.

"There is that sweet angel," Grandma Mary Belle said as she reached her hands forward to hold her.

I sat beside Grandma in case her shaky hands couldn't keep Grace Anna safe, but she never wavered while holding her close.

As I watched the two of them, my grandma became a different person. Her sometimes stern demeanor morphed into the softest, sweetest spirit. She gained so much joy from Grace Anna. She softly sang to her as she rocked her against her chest. It was as if the two of them were in their own little world.

God blessed Grace Anna with the ability to bring joy and hope to my grandma as she had to so many others throughout the world. Even though it was not going to be easy to protect her from the evil in this world, I knew the world needed her light. I knew I had to continue with her pages and posts.

After some lunch and conversation, I hugged Grandma's neck and kissed her cheek. She kissed Grace Anna's forehead. "I love you, sweet girl."

As I drove back home, I thought of all the lovely correspondence we had received over the years from people in all walks of life. People facing a wide variety of struggles gained strength from Grace Anna. How could I take a glimpse of hope away from them and allow the bullies to win?

Once we arrived home, the message light blinked on our answering machine. A few messages came from telemarketers—then one from Katrina.

"Call me when you get in. I think you'll be happy," she said.

Being the impatient person I am, I immediately typed in the website address. It was gone. Tears of joy streamed down my face. She did it! I was so excited. I didn't know how she accomplished it, but I needed to thank her.

"Hello," Katrina said.

"Thank you, thank you, thank you!" I chirped.

"You're very welcome. It took some time, but I finally got it down."

It took Katrina close to three weeks to provide enough evidence for the host company to be convinced that the site was being used for illegal harassment. I would have figured one picture would have been enough.

Katrina had managed to remove the dreadful website, but it wasn't the only place Grace Anna was being mocked and ridiculed. The biggest site we had to monitor was also the site we used the most to get her message out—Facebook.

Facebook has long protected its members' freedom of speech. I have no problem with this until it becomes threatening, bullying, or indecent. People used my daughter's images and videos as their own personal tools to try to humiliate Grace Anna and our family.

Many times, followers of Grace Anna's page would message us with info about someone creating a page with her images. I suspect it was the same person many times, someone who used the phrase "I would be better off dead " mixed with words like *troll*, *midget*, *retard*, and *moron*—words that made me shudder. I couldn't comprehend the callousness of the posts. Who thinks like that?

I also could not fathom speaking of anyone like that. It became progressively harder to remain calm in a storm devoted to trashing my young daughter. I prayed for wisdom and guidance daily about how to handle the situations. I didn't want the bullies' darkness to tarnish the joy that existed within our life.

With the help of my friend Melissa Jarboe, we discovered that some of the posts were traced to an IP address out of California. With today's technology, people have the capability to hide many aspects of their lives. The Internet is no exception. The money it would take to stop the predators was more than our family could afford, so we had to rely on Facebook to do the right thing.

Sometimes Facebook would remove them with one complaint from me. Sometimes it would take complaints from several people over many days. I could never tell what made the difference that warranted the removal. We could get some pages with only one image easily removed. Others with several videos would take weeks. Figuring out what fell under the category of abuse for Facebook confused us.

"I cannot believe this!" I yelled to Jeff. "Look at how they are portraying Grace Anna. She is a child, innocent. Why would they attack a child?"

"It's because they are empty inside. They can't understand how great she is. They have to be numb to do that toward her."

At times, a video of Grace Anna would be edited to show her making weird facial expressions with awful words scrolling across them. Other times, photos were edited with words and images. It didn't matter to me what they were. Any of it was uncalled for. It was our daughter, and children should be protected from any predator—online or otherwise.

I reviewed Facebook's Community Standards many, many times, especially the standards on bullying and harassment. They had protection of private individuals, but since Grace Anna was considered a public figure, I wondered if this extended to public pages. It should not have mattered.

I searched for a phone number for Facebook. It's been my experience when you speak to someone one-on-one, you can get more accomplished. Unfortunately, Facebook only has one way of contacting them, through the specific contact links they provide.

"Honey, you have to let this go," Jeff warned. "It's starting to take over your life."

"I know you're right, but it hurts my heart so much that something is out there putting her in that light. I feel so helpless."

He was right. Deep down I knew this quest to protect Grace Anna from online bullying consumed my thoughts. I needed to trust that God would take care of us and protect Grace Anna. I also hoped Facebook would remove the abusive pages.

As with everything good God has made, an evil version also exists, trying to rob our joy and happiness. I didn't want my family focusing energy away from living to the happiest. More than likely the cyberbullying was never going to completely stop. I couldn't spend my days engulfed in that dark world.

I limited the time I spent evaluating bullying to two hours a month. If a follower reported it, I filed it on my computer and addressed it on the set-aside hours.

"I can't change their hearts, but I can pray for them," I told Jeff.

"That's right," he replied. "And maybe one day they will see what we see in Grace Anna."

Not everyone will love us. It's a hard fact of life. We can't change who people are, but how we live our lives can be a light. We can pray for them. Deep in my heart, I knew Grace Anna's light would shine through the darkness that was aimed at her.

My time was better spent on my family and faith. My little girl faced very tough challenges that they didn't know about. Maybe someday those who wanted to hurt her will realize how amazing she is and what a warrior she really is.

15

GROWING PAINS

Before Grace Anna, I always thought I knew what being tough was all about, but I soon realized I only knew a small portion of what some people face each day. My young daughter encountered hurdles most adults never face, and at times I felt powerless to help her face those giant mountains.

One day, Grace Anna cried about her legs. "Momma, they won't stop jerking."

As she lay across my lap, I rubbed her legs back and forth, trying to get the muscle spasms to ease up. They were so intense it felt as if fireworks were going off in her legs. Grace Anna kicked and rocked her legs, continually trying to influence the muscles to relax.

"I'm here, honey. I'm here. Just breathe," I said, trying to soothe her.

Inside, my chest felt as if it would erupt with sorrow, watching her go through the pain. We questioned her doctors, but no one could give us a resolution to the cramps that didn't involve heavily sedating muscle relaxers. Grace Anna hated the way they made her feel, and I didn't want her being lifeless most of the day.

As her legs eased up, she drifted off to sleep in my arms. I stroked her hair from her face and continued to rock her in my arms, gazing at her beautiful face. She was finally at peace.

I kept wondering why she had to endure such hardships. I knew I was not supposed to question God, but the humanness in me desperately wanted to yell, "Why?"

I placed her gently in the bed and snuggled beside her. Ever since we almost lost Grace Anna after her first spine surgery, she had horrible panic attacks at night. Before the surgery, she would go to bed early and sleep all night in her crib, but after the surgery she had to have me by her side at night. It wasn't ideal, but until she was emotionally ready, I needed to comfort her.

The muscle cramps in her legs and hips had no set pattern of appearance. Grace Anna had wonderful days most weeks, but when she had a bad day, it took quite a bit out of her. The normally sunshiny girl turned understandably cranky and impatient. Tylenol and Advil can only do so much. Back problems are very hard to treat, especially in children. We had to find ways to help her cope with the pain and still enjoy her life.

Finding therapists that meshed with Grace Anna's personality and needs was not an easy task. With the rarity of Conradi-Hünermann syndrome, few therapists knew much about the disorder. If they didn't understand how her body grew and the complications that went along with it, they possibly could make her health worse. We had few options. In the rural community in which we live, there is no pediatric therapist. We had to search in towns at least forty minutes from our home.

We started out in a larger, more well-known facility, but she rarely saw the same therapist. Grace Anna couldn't bond with any therapist. Then we heard of Kids Can Do in Danville, Kentucky. We were very fortunate to find two very good therapists who also cared deeply for Grace Anna and our family.

Physical therapy greatly helped Grace Anna manage her pain, gain strength, and learn to use her body to function every day. Joanna started working with Grace Anna at age two. When we first started, Grace Anna could not sit up on her own due to the weakening of her muscles caused by the casting.

Joanna had a personality much like my own. She was tough when she needed to be, but tender when Grace Anna required it. She believed Grace Anna was capable of much more than sitting in her wheelchair, an attitude I looked for in a therapist. I knew in my heart my daughter would walk, maybe not like everyone else, but she would walk. Joanna felt the same.

"Up, Grace Anna! You can do it," Joanna cheered, trying to motivate her. "Three more."

"I'm tired, Miss Joanna. I can't do it," Grace Anna replied.

"Yes, you can. Do one and we'll rest, then finish the last two."

The more Grace Anna wanted to quit, the more Joanna created new ways to motivate her to do her physical therapy. Joanna also taught me valuable exercises I could do with Grace Anna at home. These helped when her muscles tensed up and also strengthened them. The hour of therapy greatly improved Grace Anna's quality of life. It also educated me with methods to be the best caregiver for Grace Anna.

Once Grace Anna finished her hour of physical therapy, it was time for occupational therapy. Ellen had a different personality than Joanna. She was somewhat softer with her direction but still structured. Occupational therapy is often viewed as helping people function at a job, but it actually helps in their entire environment.

Ellen instructed Grace Anna on dressing herself. "Grab with both your hands and pull your head through."

Grace Anna poked her arm through the arm hole. "Miss Ellen, this is driving me crazy."

Ellen showed a great amount of patience, watching Grace Anna miss the hole several times, but she never became negative. "You've got it. Keep trying."

Grace Anna struggled with dressing herself due to the weakness in her core, the way her arms grew, and the overall size of her trunk. It didn't help that her legs wouldn't allow her to bend to get her bottoms on. Trying to get her legs to do something they were not structurally equipped to do frustrated her.

This meant Ellen had to educate her on different ways to maneuver her body to complete daily life skills that come easily to others. Even though Grace Anna struggled with the skills, she worked hard as Ellen encouraged her. Some moments I wanted to run over and help her, but I knew Grace Anna ached to gain independence and to be her own person.

Over the next four years, Joanna and Ellen worked tirelessly to provide Grace Anna with wonderful therapy. Every time a surgery would set back her progress, they would redesign their approach to get Grace Anna on the road to recovery. Grace Anna had fought her way to be able to walk with her walker, ride a tricycle, and perform routines to help her become independent in many aspects of her life.

Then came the day that broke our hearts. Joanna took a new position at a different facility. It had taken so long to find someone Grace Anna could connect with. After discussing it with her pediatrician and praying about it, we decided as a family to give her a fresh start at a new facility, Total Pediatrics.

Michael and Laura have been working with Grace Anna since December of 2016, and it has been wonderful. It's early in the therapy process, but we have already seen improvements, and Grace Anna has connected with both beautifully. I fully believe they will be an important part of Grace Anna's ability to become completely independent one day.

Even though therapy was helpful, it did not solve all the issues of living with Conradi-Hünermann syndrome. She still struggled with being outside in the heat, to the point of breaking into a full panic whenever temperatures rose above eighty degrees. Hives would break out across her neck and back. She couldn't enjoy playing outside until the evening hours. Then we had to combat bugs.

We grappled with ideas that would give her time outside, and then the idea of a pool came up. Doctors felt aquatic therapy was a good option for Grace Anna's therapy, and other kids with Conradi had improved greatly with aquatic therapy.

Pools were very expensive and time consuming to maintain, but purchasing our own was a better option than taking her to public pools. Something about public pools caused problems with her health. We tried some facilities in other counties, but she always ended up at the doctor after going to one.

Once the pool was up and running, Grace Anna was in her own little piece of heaven. "Look at me, Momma. I'm swimming," she exclaimed. "Woo-hoo! I'm having so much fun."

The pool gave her freedom to go outside, plus it helped strengthen her body. The water put less stress on her body, making it easier for her to exercise. It also gave us time to be together as a family and enjoy ourselves. It has been by far one of the best investments we have made for her life.

As time flew by, one thing never changed: Grace Anna wanted the rod out of her back. Her tiny body could barely encase the rod protruding on her back. It looked painful, and she didn't like anyone coming near it.

"Momma, please take the rod out of my back. It feels like it's going to burst through my skin."

"I wish I could, baby. We just can't. It may happen someday, but it's not right now," I tried explaining to her.

"No, I want it out!" she insisted. "Mom it hurts, and it won't move."

I wanted to rip the rod out. I wanted to wave a magic wand over her back and make her spine straight and the rod disappear, but I didn't have that power. It was maddening to listen to her cry out in pain and know there was nothing I could do for her except listen, soothe, and pray.

We prayed and prayed and prayed.

Every night Grace Anna prayed for God to touch her body.

"Please Lord, take the rod out of my back. It hurts, and I don't want it."

I prayed the same, asking God to strengthen her body so she could become independent and pain-free. At times, it felt as if my prayers made it to the ceiling, then bounced off. I wanted to run, I wanted to shout, I wanted someone to stop and see she was hurting. I wanted someone to acknowledge that her life wasn't easy, but she would one day live without physical pain and anguish.

It wasn't too much to ask, I thought. She was a light to so many, but did they really know what she faced every day? Did they know when she first awoke each morning, we had to work her legs to get them going? Did they even care?

I couldn't see the bitterness building up in me, but everyone in my family could.

"I'm so tired of hearing how their kid didn't get in the ball game or their kid had hurt feelings because a friend didn't say hello," I complained. "Seriously, do they even have a clue what we go through? What Grace Anna goes through? Do they think I want to hear about all the trivial junk they're dealing with?"

"Yes, Mom, they do." Isaiah looked at me, disheartened.

"He's right," Jeff added. "They love their kids and what they experience is big to them. They don't know what she faces, and even if they did, they would never truly understand it unless they went through it. Would you have realized it before Grace Anna?"

Guilt for feeling this way hit me, but in my head, I felt justified. Grace Anna shone her sweet smile everywhere, and no one had any idea how tough she really was. It hurt me that people were not empathetic enough to think before they started complaining to me. How dare they!

Then God reminded me of life before Grace Anna. The days when my life was about coaching, teaching, and living a life on the go. Jeff and I played volleyball and did whatever we wanted without a care in the world. The days when I thought if Isaiah lost a baseball game, I would have a convulsion. Life before a child with severe health issues. It was a very different life, and I would have been one of those people complaining if Isaiah didn't get to play first base that day.

"You're both right," I said, with tears welling up in my eyes.

I knew they were right, but it didn't ease the pain of watching Grace Anna hurt. Seeing a kid running or watching a group of girls throw around a baseball hurt my heart. It weighed heavily that she missed things in life. I should have known Grace Anna had a life full of love, support, and adventure. The only one stressing over it was me.

I had allowed negativity to rear its ugly head. I knew better. I knew God had an awesome plan for her, even if I didn't understand it all. I knew her pain would make her stronger and able to face things that would come at her in life. I once again had to give up trying to control our situation. I had to rely on God.

Grace Anna was the one dealing with the pain and struggle. I was a bystander, trying my best to help her, along with Jeff and Isaiah. They too had to deal with seeing her struggles, and both stayed positive 99 percent of the time, which was quite annoying at times. But they were right. Time for me to let go of my bitterness and envy and refocus my attention on helping Grace Anna the best I could.

I felt in my soul that Grace Anna would someday get an answer to her prayer. She would live without the rod and step out on faith with her own two feet without any help from anyone except God. I didn't know then that a miracle was in the making, and Grace Anna would see one of her prayers answered sooner than any of us expected.

16

NAVIGATING THE OPEN SEA

Grace Anna's popularity grew, and the requests for her to perform came rolling in. The toughest part was choosing what was best for Grace Anna so she could have a normal childhood and remain healthy. We never wanted her life to be a show or for her to feel pressured to do what a stranger asked.

We were offered a part in a new TV series that was getting programming together for the pilot. It started out very positive—something our family thought we could be a part of. The producer had a very welcoming personality and loved talking with me every week. I felt I had researched her enough for our family to make a commitment to the show.

Then she began avoiding my phone calls, and things she had arranged kept falling through. A singing opportunity with a popular group fell through, and she repeated some harsh things the group had allegedly said about Grace Anna. Jeff and I realized we had made a big mistake trusting the woman.

Then a phone call came from Katrina, who had helped us with the Internet bullying.

Katrina relayed, "I got a phone call today from a lady saying you would promise concerts with Grace Anna in exchange for me building up her IMDb status."

The IMDb (Internet Movie Database) is devoted to information on celebrities and entertainment. It seemed the producer thought it was good to promote herself by using Grace Anna. I felt sick to my stomach. How naïve I had been. She knew exactly how to play me. I trusted someone I never should have.

"What part do you not understand?" I asked when I called her. "How is it appropriate for you to be contacting a mutual acquaintance, promising her we will do things you've never discussed with me?"

"I was going to tell you about it, but I've been busy."

"I think it would be best if we parted ways. We're concerned you are more interested in self-promotion than what is best for our daughter. We do not want Grace Anna's life used as a tool. She is a little girl, not a product."

The conversation did not go much smoother after that, and it took a few weeks to finally break ties with the producer.

After that experience, I interacted with people interested in Grace Anna's story with extreme caution. From then on, I had to realize not everyone was genuine, not everyone was a Christian, and we were going to have to pray for guidance every time we were offered an opportunity for Grace Anna and our family.

Money was never a factor to us deciding what to take part in. We never wanted Grace Anna to be the bread and butter of our family finances. Jeff and I were her parents, and we would provide for her. We also never wanted to take part in anything that went against our beliefs and morals.

Our family has always been very supportive of our veterans and active military. We consider them to be the best of America, giving their lives to protect our country and ensure we keep our freedom. I was beyond excited when Melissa Jarboe of the Military Veteran Project contacted us, requesting that Grace Anna sing for our soldiers and their families.

Melissa started Military Veteran Project in honor of her husband, Jamie Jarboe, who died from injuries sustained in Afghanistan. Melissa left her corporate position to start the organization with her own money. She formed it to help soldiers battling post-traumatic stress syndrome and to help prevent suicide in veterans and active soldiers through research and treatment.

Once Melissa and I discussed the ins and outs of the request, Grace Anna was set to sing the national anthem at the upcoming Salute to Our Hero's Gala in Topeka, Kansas. It was very exciting for us as a family to be part of honoring our veterans.

"Dad would have been so proud," Jeff said.

"I know. He would have loved it. My grandparents would have loved it also."

Melissa and I became very close during the time between the scheduling of the event and the actual day. I learned what her husband endured while serving our country. Jamie became paralyzed from the chest down after being shot by a sniper in Afghanistan. He spent many days in and out of hospitals, trying to recover. Unfortunately, Jamie died less than a year after being shot.

Melissa promised Jamie she would do whatever she could to help his fellow soldiers make it through excruciating times in their lives. Melissa was touched by Grace Anna's zest for life and patriotism. It warmed my heart to know Grace Anna's life had made an impression on a lady who had made such a difference for our veterans.

November approached and try as I might, Grace Anna would not practice singing the anthem. I imagined her getting up onstage, starting to sing, but not knowing the words. I tried begging, bribing, and singing it myself, but she wasn't buying into it.

Grace Anna acted as if it was any other day of her singing. But for me to think she could get up there and not sing racked my nerves.

"Grace Anna, let's practice it one more time."

"No, Momma, I don't want to."

"Do you want to sing tomorrow?"

Grace Anna looked at me with her eyes wide open. "Mom, yes, I want to sing. I know the song."

As hard as it was to believe a four-year-old girl could realize she was ready for a very important performance, she didn't seem very nervous. But Jeff, Isaiah, and I sure were.

Never mind that Colonel Ernest Garcia would be there—he worked with former President Reagan and was a very highly decorated veteran. Bobby Henline would also be there. Bobby was a highly decorated veteran, living with terrible injuries he incurred while defending our country. He now toured the country as a comedian to help other soldiers and veterans. Many soldiers and their families would be there too. I knew the day would be important for them.

I wanted it to go as wonderfully as possible, but she was just a little girl. Was all this pressure necessary? No. Why was I stressing out so much? She was four. Grace Anna knew she was prepared. It would be fine. Right?

We arrived at a beautifully decorated hall full of distinguished veterans and soldiers along with their families. We were seated with Colonel Garcia, his wife, and Bobby Henline. We had wonderful conversation with each of them. Melissa stopped by to check on us.

"How is everyone doing?" she asked.

"Fine. I just hope she doesn't get up there and freeze."

Melissa tried to comfort us. "She will be fine. If she stops, everyone will understand."

I sure hoped so.

Then the moment arrived. After a lovely introduction, we made our way to the stage.

"Grace Anna. They said my name, Grace Anna!" It surprised her someone was saying her name so loudly.

Grace Anna grabbed the microphone, turned to the front of the room, and belted out the anthem with such passion and intensity it shook my core. I could not believe she had not sung the song in over four months. She delivered a powerhouse performance. I stood in awe of our amazing little girl.

She finished to a loud roar of cheers and clapping. Her little body shook with excitement. She did it. She knew all along she would knock it out of the park. Hearing how it touched the soldiers' hearts was even more gratifying. What a joy to see these decorated veterans and soldiers ask to take selfies with our girl. She had no idea what an amazing thing she had done.

We spent more time with Melissa and her family, enjoying our visit and getting to know each other better. It seemed as if our families had known each other forever. It was a great experience we will never forget. It also restored our faith that people full of integrity and respect for Grace Anna and our family still existed.

Three months later Grace Anna was invited to sing the national anthem at the Illinois Call to Prayer Caucus. Senator Sam McCann was a very humble man from humble beginnings in West Virginia. He moved to Illinois to live with his wife, Vicki, and their two children, determined to make a difference for the state of Illinois.

Through several phone discussions and emails, we agreed to allow Grace Anna to participate. Prayer is a powerful part of our lives. Anything that promoted prayer was a plus to us.

It was a very cold February day when we arrived in Springfield. Vicki greeted us at the capitol and welcomed us into Senator McCann's office. We toured the capitol and took pictures with Grace Anna in the governor's office. As with Melissa Jarboe, Senator McCann and Vicki felt like family. The level of comfort was astonishing since we barely knew each other.

Grace Anna also felt so at ease. Once again, she refused to practice. I finally quit worrying about it. What would be, would be. I decided to relax and live in the moment.

"I'm so glad you're here, Grace Anna," Vicki said, reaching out to hug her.

Grace Anna normally will not hug perfect strangers, but she reached straight out to Vicki. "Hi, I'm Grace Anna," she said. "Nice to meet you."

We all laughed together. She was becoming quite the little entertainer. It did not bother her at all to meet new people or be in front of crowds. Grace Anna had a gift to connect to others by being herself, and she could tell when someone was genuine.

As we gathered in the capitol building with citizens, senators, and representatives, the mind-set impressed me. It was strictly about prayer. No arguing or negativity intruded. Everyone focused on bringing a positive change to Illinois.

After a few speakers, Senator McCann briefly introduced Grace Anna. We approached the microphone, and Grace Anna froze.

Oh no, I thought. *What are we going to do?*

All I could think to do was sing. I softly sang, and Grace Anna kicked right in. I don't know why, but at that moment she wasn't ready. Once she realized what was going on, she took over the performance.

When she finished singing, a crowd of adoring fans greeted her. She loved the attention, but I could sense she was tired and needed a break.

Vicki wrapped her arm around me. "She did an awesome job. Let's go eat."

I was so glad she asked. We were ready to eat and needed to take a breath to be a family.

The slight miscue made Grace Anna even more adorable. It also gave her a chance to see if she ever messed up, everything would still be okay. It also helped Jeff and I to back off on the performances and let her be a kid for a while.

Life had been moving so swiftly that we never thought of how it would affect Grace Anna. She was used to a daily schedule and being home. We were still glad she had the opportunities to perform at events, but we decided to limit her appearances until she was older and her health was more stable.

Grace Anna's light had once again brought people into our lives that we more than likely would have never met. People we now consider part of our family.

Melissa Jarboe is one of my dearest friends now and has been by our sides during some very trying times during Grace Anna's surgeries. She also visits our home, and we talk monthly about things going on in our lives. She has given us sound advice in dealing with being in the limelight. I trust her judgment and am grateful for her friendship and family.

Senator McCann and his wife, Vicki, also remain close friends with our family. They have been a constant reminder that some people in the political realm are genuinely good people, seeking to do the best they can for our country. They, along with their children, are in our prayers daily as we are also in theirs.

Many more experiences have come our way as we've supported Grace Anna's performances. We never charged for performances, but we always told people we'd be grateful for whatever God laid on their hearts to give. We never felt using our daughter's performances to gain money was appropriate. If someone wanted to help, we would rather they do it from the goodness of their hearts. One of those experiences included a church in our home state with a very big heart.

We were honored when Grace Anna was asked to sing at Southland Christian Church in Lexington, Kentucky. Their representative, Kim, asked, "What do you normally charge for an appearance?"

"Whatever God lays upon your hearts," I replied. "We do not have a specific fee for appearances."

Grace Anna loved singing at the event, and the people were amazing. Pastor Jon Weece was very welcoming and doted on Grace Anna. They surprised us with a donation to cover the installation of a central heat and air system for our home. It was a testament to an answered prayer. They already had an amount decided before Grace Anna ever performed. God blessed us as Grace Anna blessed them through her story and singing.

Grace Anna could touch the world from home through her Facebook page and YouTube. We didn't have to travel all over the world to allow her to be an inspiration. She needed to be a little girl too. She could still participate in events, but only the ones that greatly touched our hearts. We never wanted her childhood to be about providing income for our family; her childhood was about her being a child like all other children in the world.

I already knew Grace Anna was changing the world through her music, love of life, and story. In the years to come, she would continue to change me and help our family, especially Isaiah, deal with a whole heap of hurt.

17

BROTHER AND SISTER

There are people in life that forever change how you view the world. My son, Isaiah, is one of those people.

Isaiah was four years old when his dad left. Looking back, I wish I had handled some things differently. My faith was not as strong then, and my fear of being a single mom got to me at times. I tried my best to shield him from the pain of events that can sometimes take place during a divorce, but I will admit I messed up sometimes.

He became very close to me and did not like me to leave him much. I ached when he left with his dad every other weekend, but he needed time with him. A lot of adapting needed to occur to get our lives back to some sort of normalcy. I wasn't sure how to do it.

I spent many nights awake at 2:00 a.m. in tears, praying for God to help me. I was so overwhelmed. Should I quit school or finish my degree? If I had quit, Isaiah would have learned to give up, and I couldn't be a quitter, especially when my son needed me to be a fighter.

My precious great aunt Shirley was an angel on earth for Isaiah and me. She would drive to our home every morning through the week and take care of Isaiah while I finished my teaching degree at Eastern Kentucky University. She also basically took care of me.

"You are his world now. Show him that life can be great again," she said to me. "One day when you look back on this, you will realize it has made you a better, stronger woman."

I would come home to supper made, my house spotless, and my son happy. Her encouragement and compassion for Isaiah and me have been one of the treasures I hold dear in my heart. She was one of my favorite people I ever knew.

Once I finished college, I was very fortunate to obtain a teaching position my first summer after graduating. I was very passionate about teaching. I loved seeing students learn something new while doing a cool science experiment. The school was very accommodating for a single mother. I didn't have to worry about finding a sitter to watch Isaiah if school was cancelled. I could stay home with him.

After moving to Russell County to be closer to my school, Isaiah was very fortunate to be a student at the Little Learning Center and Salem Elementary. I could not have asked for a better educational experience than what was provided at those schools. Isaiah also made lifelong friends, and we became part of a loving and helpful community.

We also started attending Ono Community Church. Some of Isaiah's teachers went there as well as some of my colleagues. When I began my master's program through Eastern Kentucky University, one teacher took Isaiah under her wing and took care of him while I completed my classes. Mary Beth was possibly the sweetest person I became friends with in Russell County. She walked the walk as a Christian woman and was an excellent person for my son to be around.

The community known as Gosser Ridge was home to us for a long time. Isaiah was happy, but something was still missing. His letter to Santa his kindergarten year of school made it clear exactly what he wanted.

My colleague at school kept asking me, "A man, huh?"

I had no idea what he was talking about, but evidently it was something very funny.

"Have you seen the letters to Santa in the newspaper?" he asked.

"No, why?"

"Here you go." He handed me the paper, and there it was in black and white for the entire county to read.

At first, I was mortified, because I knew some of my friends would never let me live it down. It appeared as if I was desperate for a man, and I most definitely was not. At that point in my life, I wasn't very concerned with ever getting married again. My feelings of being mortified turned into a feeling of heartbrokenness for my son.

He had written his letter to Santa, asking for the usual stuff a six-year-old boy would ask for: a Batman, some baseballs, a basketball, games, and a train set. Then came the very last line, "Please bring my mommy a man."

To many it would seem he wanted me to have someone to replace his dad in our home. That wasn't the case. Even though his dad and I were not married anymore, I always taught Isaiah to respect his dad and love him. I didn't agree completely with Freddie on everything, but I was not going to run him down to Isaiah. That doesn't help anyone.

This was about a dream of Isaiah's to have a sibling. He had been asking me for over a year for a brother or sister. I always replied, "I have to be married again before you can have a sibling."

That afternoon, I picked him up from school and kissed his precious forehead. "I read your letter to Santa."

His head immediately tilted down to the floor. "Mom, I just wanted somebody to help us."

"It's okay. If that's what you want, for me to meet someone and maybe someday to get a brother or sister, that is what I'll try to do."

He took it to heart. In his innocent mind, the best way for him to get a brother or sister was to ask Santa for help. He had prayed for a sibling for years. He would see his friends hanging out with their brothers, and he went home to just his momma. It crushed me. He never asked for much from me, but he wanted a sibling desperately.

The hurt of divorce can damage how we view the world sometimes. It had turned me against the thought of marriage again, but when I became a mom, I made a vow to Isaiah that his childhood would be the best I could possibly make it. I realized I needed to entertain the possibility that I could fall in love again, spend my life with someone, and have more children. He and I both needed it. He also needed to see what a strong marriage was. Our kids grow to be much like us. I never wanted him to experience the hurt of a divorce as an adult. I would take the plunge and try to date again.

When Jeff and I met and married, the hope of having more children seemed a possibility. But after the three miscarriages, we were spiritually exhausted. Yet, my heart knew Isaiah still dreamed of having a sibling. He has this great big heart that loves everyone. I've never met anyone like him. He has the most tender spirit, and he had so much to offer a sibling. I ached to give him that chance.

Throughout my pregnancy, Isaiah would come to my bedroom at night and lay his hand on my belly and pray for Grace Anna. He maintained a positive attitude the entire pregnancy.

"Mom, this baby is going to make it," he would say.

I've never seen a child so excited to have a sibling. It was endearing.

Then Grace Anna arrived and Isaiah fell in love.

The moment he held Grace Anna the first time, she stole his heart. Tears streamed down his chubby cheeks as he grinned from ear to ear. "Momma, she's beautiful."

I rubbed the tears from his cheeks and kissed his forehead. "You both are my miracles," I said. "I'm the luckiest momma on this planet."

That's when a revelation hit my soul: here sat my gentle giant holding my tiny warrior. They were made for each other. So many years lay between them, and their sizes differed greatly, but deep in my spirit I knew their relationship was special. Their differences would complement each other, and they would bring out the best in each other. A prayer had not only been answered for Jeff and me, one was answered for Isaiah.

Having a baby at thirty-seven was quite a bit harder to recover from than when I had Isaiah at twenty-four. My first few weeks home, I struggled to get back on my feet. Isaiah must have sensed how hard it was recuperating, so he took things into his own hands. He would get up before he had to leave for school, feed Grace Anna her first bottle of the morning, change her diaper, and put her back to bed, leaving me to rest. For a thirteen-year-old boy to take the initiative to take care of us amazed me.

"You rest, Momma. I've got her," he would say. He was such a natural with her. He wasn't nervous picking her up or changing her. He loved her so much. Watching him care for her filled me with joy. Grace Anna was very fortunate to be given a brother that not only wanted to be a good big brother but someone determined to see her have the best life ever.

Isaiah has always been a laid-back person. In his years on this earth, I have seldom seen him lose his temper or be angry with anyone. He has the ability to love people many would deem unlovable. He truly tries to find the best in people.

In the first few years of Grace Anna's life, if Isaiah wasn't at one of his ball games, he was at home helping us out. He loved interacting with Grace Anna. If I went to get groceries, he went with us. On a trip to a local Kroger, the calm son I had always known turned completely livid over a can of pickles.

"Mom, I cannot believe this!" he yelled.

"Isaiah, honey, calm down. What is wrong?"

"Mom, look. How in the world could they put that on a pickle jar?" Tears welled up in his eyes.

I grabbed the jar of pickles, and there it was. The most dreaded word people with dwarfism hear and see: *midget*. A look of complete frustration swept over Isaiah's face as he held a jar of pickles. I had no idea where to begin. I hated the word as much as he did, but sometimes we must choose our battles when standing up for Grace Anna.

"Isaiah, they are pickles," I said. "They aren't calling your sister that."

"But Mom, it's not right. How can it be okay for them to put this on a jar for everyone to see?"

"Sometimes things in the past that seemed right at the time are not now," I explained. "The best thing we can do is educate, not hate."

Once we returned home, we researched the word together, learned why the term was used, and discussed ways we could look out for Grace Anna while educating others. He began to feel better about the situation. He had a plan now when people said the word or he saw it in literature. If he saw it in advertisements or on products, he could write the company, citing reasons to avoid using the word. If people said it in front of him, he learned not to become angry but to calmly explain why the word was inappropriate.

When Isaiah entered eighth grade, we felt as a family it would be better if he transferred to our home county school. At first he was reluctant, but once he realized he had family at the school, he agreed. He fit in quite well, joining the basketball and baseball teams and making new friends. Grace Anna even had the opportunity to see some of his basketball games.

Then she had surgery at the hospital. We expected to be home within a week from the surgery, but once it was clear she was struggling to recover, we had another problem. What were we going to do with Isaiah? He could stay with his dad some, but he lived two counties away. My sister and her family welcomed him into their home the entire month we were gone. It was a very hard time on Isaiah. He called several times, worried about Grace Anna.

I felt as if I had abandoned him. Thankfully my niece and nephew along with his friends helped occupy his time while we were gone. Each night I would update him on Grace Anna's progress, listen to things going on at home, and pray for concerns we had.

Once we arrived home from Baltimore, he hovered over Grace Anna for weeks, making sure she was comfortable, feeding her supper, and playing with her. One thing they loved to do together was spin Grace Anna like a top.

When Grace Anna came home from Baltimore, Isaiah was the

provider of entertainment. He came up with ways to keep her mind off how her body was confined to her cast. His ability to make her laugh not only helped her but provided moments I will cherish the rest of my life, seeing my two children in complete adoration of each other.

Isaiah spent many days entertaining her while she recovered in the cast. He danced, he sang, he played with stuffed animals—whatever she wanted him to do, he did it. It was apparent she had him wrapped around her little pinky, and he loved every minute of it.

I cherished the moments when they spent time together being brother and sister. I figured eventually Isaiah would distance himself from her, since he was getting closer to being an adult, but as the years progressed, their bond grew.

He still helped with her care and spent time playing with her. When he came home from a late game, he marched straight to her room to check on her. His level of concern for his sister was very rare for a boy his age.

He's never been jealous of her popularity or the amount of attention she was paid. He hates the limelight, hates getting up in front of people to speak. He would rather talk to someone one-on-one than a crowd of people.

He was so confident in who he was that he did not feel the need to act out or be aggressive for our attention. It got to me, at times, though. People would ask about Grace Anna, brag on Grace Anna, and act like Isaiah didn't exist. It infuriated me. He was such a gem, but people sometimes overlook the quiet, strong individuals that help everyone else achieve things.

I made it a point to brag on him as much as I bragged on Grace Anna. They were both my children, both were very special, and both had a God-given purpose to make this world a better place.

While Isaiah looked out for Grace Anna, he himself suffered several health issues. His freshman year he tore a ligament in his arm while pitching in a high school baseball game. He heard it pop, but continued to pitch because he didn't want to let his team down. What he didn't understand was the more he pitched that day, the more it injured his ligament. He ended up having ligament replacement surgery.

As he rested in his bed during recovery, guess who snuggled up beside him? Grace Anna of course. She tried her best to ease his pain. She even tried adjusting his brace to where she thought it would make him feel better. It was endearing to see her look out for him as he had been looking out for her.

The Christmas Isaiah turned sixteen, Jeff wanted to surprise him with a truck. Jeff isn't one to be all soft and gooey most times, but he felt Isaiah had been such a good kid, he needed rewarding. It wasn't a fancy new truck, but it was new to Isaiah, and he loved it.

Unfortunately, seven months later he slid off the wet roads and flipped his beautiful truck two times before it rested upside down. Only a small section remained uncrushed where he was sitting. He spent the evening in the hospital with a slashed elbow and banged-up body, but no severe injuries. His truck, on the other hand, was totaled.

When Isaiah returned home from the hospital, Grace Anna attended to his injuries, inspecting his cuts, helping bandage him up, and hugging him as needed.

"Momma, he's hurt," she cried as she patted his back. "Help him."

In the same way Isaiah cared for her, Grace Anna looked out for her brother. She prayed for him at night and checked on him every morning until he got to moving around better.

Between the two of them, my ability to cope with the never-ending cycle of surgeries and injuries were getting to me. I tried not to question why we were going through such rough periods, but my humaneness got the best of me sometimes.

I was also concerned it was getting to Isaiah. He had started getting sick quite a bit. His stomach ached, and he couldn't eat. We went to specialists to check out his gall bladder and stomach. His gall bladder was not functioning fully, but it did not explain all his symptoms. After a scope of his stomach, doctors were at a loss as to what was going on.

Our family doctor suggested he see an allergist. Isaiah had suffered outdoor allergies for some time, but she thought foods might also be causing some of his health issues. Boy, was she right. After the results came in, we discovered he was highly allergic to ten foods. Some he ate every day, his favorites. It crushed him to find out he would have to give up his fried potatoes with onions.

It was a lifestyle change for him and one more thing as a family we would have to take in account when planning meals. Wouldn't you know Grace Anna was allergic to some of the same foods, so it was easier to address the issue of what to fix for meals.

As the months went by, life continued to calm down a little for us, and my two children were getting closer each day. Whether it was fishing in our pond, swinging on the porch, or watching a movie together, Grace Anna and Isaiah spent valuable time together, enjoying each other's company. They continued to be each other's protector and supporter. Grace Anna was his biggest cheerleader at basketball and baseball games, while Isaiah supported her at singing and speaking events.

Isaiah was never one to want the limelight, but there were times he was part of it. He was recognized for his acts of kindness and humbleness by former Super Bowl Champion Diyral Briggs. Briggs surpised Isaiah at his high school to present him with gifts and an award for character. It was a moment Isaiah will never forget. In the hustle of life, it's easy to forget how wonderful a brother he was, never jealous or self-serving. He deserved a little recognition of his own.

We all gathered together each night before bed and reflected on the day, each of us voicing things on our minds and things we needed to pray about. Sometimes Isaiah would lead the prayer, other times Grace Anna would. We focused on the most important things in our lives. It was the most valuable time in our day, and I looked forward to it.

God had been so good to us. All those trials we went through drew us closer, but the bond between Grace Anna and Isaiah had grown tremendously. They both finally got through very tough health battles, and life was finally a little easier. But as I've learned, those periods of rest prepare us for times of intense battle.

God put two incredible children in my life, and they both made me a better person. He also knew they would help each other through difficult times. We didn't know at that time how their love for each other would help Isaiah through some of the darkest times in his life.

18

LOVE HEALS OLD WOUNDS

T imes come in life that seem so dark you wonder if you'll ever feel joy again. Moments also come in which you make mistakes that haunt you most of your life if you allow them to.

I had dated a guy named Chris my last two years of high school. He was very cute and charming, and I had the confidence of a snail. Even with all the activities I was involved with in high school, I still felt as if I was beneath my peers.

I felt ugly, fat, and unattractive.

This was a perfect setup for allowing heartache to rule my life.

Chris was not a mean guy, just young and determined to make not-so-wise decisions—same as me.

All through high school, I remained a virgin and was proud of it. I became a Christian right before my thirteenth birthday, and I took it very seriously. I didn't cuss, smoke, or drink, and I was not going to be having sex. I had been warned by my mother of the consequences of choosing to share that part of myself outside of marriage. It wasn't a good idea.

But my eighteen-year-old brain could only focus on the overwhelming adoration I felt for Chris. I chose to do something that not only disappointed myself but let down God.

One month later I was pregnant.

I couldn't believe it. I examined the pregnancy tests over and over, and they still showed I was carrying a little one.

I was not happy about it. I feared telling my parents, and shame over what I had done crushed me. Not only would I know I made a decision against my faith, everyone else would know too.

I didn't entrust anyone with the news except Chris. A month went by, and I had told no one. It ate me up inside, and I had no idea how to take care of myself or my baby. I had to tell someone. I chose my sister, Bobbie.

She was shocked, to say the least. "What are you going to do?"

"I have no idea." I would not get an abortion. I didn't believe in them, but I wasn't ready to be a mom. How could I take care of a baby when I didn't even have my own home, I wasn't married, and Chris was even more immature than I was?

I dreaded disappointing my parents, but I was getting close to ten weeks. I knew I needed to go to a doctor. The night I decided to tell my parents, something happened to my body. I was hurting badly and had spotted blood.

I was mortified. I didn't want to be a mom yet, but I still wanted my child to be okay.

Please God, don't take my baby, I begged. *I'm sorry I messed up. Please don't take it.*

After pleading with God not to take my unborn child, I picked up the phone. "Mom, please come home. I need to go to the doctor."

"Why, what's wrong?"

"I'm pregnant."

I didn't hear another word. Fifteen minutes later she arrived, and we were on our way to the hospital.

An exam and ultrasound later, I was informed my baby did not have a heartbeat. I was sent home to miscarry.

The next day, with my sister holding my hand, I miscarried my first baby in my childhood home. I had to have a D&C later that day, and the world as I had known it became a very dark and dreary place.

It broke my dad's heart and changed how my parents thought of me. It changed how I thought about myself. When I looked in the mirror, all I saw was a worthless failure. I had nothing to offer anyone. My heart was broken.

Guilt that I had ever thought of not wanting my baby plagued my mind. How could I have thought such a thing? The baby was a part of me. How could I not want to be a mom?

This guilt and self-destruction grew. Chris and I split up, and I continued to make poor decisions. I allowed men to treat me badly and tried to cope with the pain by drinking alcohol. I quit praying and quit church.

Why would anyone want to be around me? I was an embarrassment to myself and my family. What I didn't understand in my early twenties was that God loved me and would forgive me if I asked, but I continued to punish myself.

Life moved on, and I married Isaiah's dad. After Isaiah was born, I started going back to a wonderful church in Bethelridge, Kentucky. I sought redemption from the Lord and grew stronger in my Christian faith, but a part of me still held onto the guilt.

When Freddie and I divorced, a part of me felt I deserved the heartache. After all the time that had passed, I still had not let go of the guilt. I had just accepted that I had messed up my life, and I would be lucky if I would ever be fully happy again.

I never shared my past mistakes with many people, but I wanted Jeff to know everything about me—the good, the bad, and the ugly. If he accepted it all, maybe I could finally move on.

I did for a short time.

With each miscarriage we experienced, an accusing voice in my head pounded the idea that my unborn children now suffered because I had messed up all those years ago. How foolish I was.

After the birth of Grace Anna, I was so focused on taking care of her, I didn't have the time to ponder things that happened over twenty years before.

Then Grace Anna spoke. She spoke about something she had never been told about. She spoke of her brothers and sisters in heaven.

"Momma," Grace Anna said. "Do I have sisters?"

"What? You have your brother, Isaiah."

"No, I mean my sisters in heaven. I saw them, Mom."

How could this be? We had made sure she didn't know anything about the miscarriages. What was going on? Had she seen a vision from God? I didn't know what to think, but I decided to tell her about them.

"Yes, Peanut, you have four siblings in heaven," I told her. "Mommy carried them in her belly, and they went on to be with Jesus before you were born."

"I saw them. They are beautiful."

With all my might, I fought the tears welling in my eyes, but they streamed down my cheeks anyway.

Grace Anna brushed them off my face. "Momma, they are okay."

Cold chills covered my body. I fully believe God sends messages through children and adults. I held onto her words and trusted all my children were safe and happy with God.

A few months later I dreamed of the children I miscarried. Three girls dressed in soft white gowns with long curly blonde hair were holding hands amid beautiful scenery. They smiled and laughed. They were different ages and heights.

The tallest daughter turned to me. "Let us go, Momma. We are okay."

I couldn't see myself in the dream—just their beautiful faces. But someone was missing. I looked around for my fourth child, who was nowhere in sight.

The three girls climbed into beautifully made beds and rested their heads.

As I searched to find my fourth child, I began to panic in my dream. Was this child lost? What had happened?

Then I felt a tug on my left arm. It was him looking up at me with large dark-brown eyes. "I'm right here, Momma."

He had been holding my hand the entire time. I felt such sorrow in the dream. "I'm so sorry," I told him. "I love you so much. I want to see you so much."

He smiled at me. His curly brown hair lay gently across the edge of his face. He looked like an angel. Peace came over me as I held his precious hand. I couldn't imagine ever letting it go, then he began releasing his hand from mine. I tried with all my might to grip as tightly as I could to keep him near me. I had waited so long to be with them; I didn't want to lose them again. The dream felt so real. I knew they were my children. God had sent me a moment to be with them.

"Please don't go!" I yelled. "I need you to stay. I love you all so much."

But he continued to walk over beside his sisters. All four of them smiled at me with looks of peace and happiness. I wanted to run to them, but my body wouldn't move. I tried yelling at them, but no sound came from my mouth.

They all joined together and grabbed each other's hands. With a glowing light above their heads, they said in unison, "Momma, let us go. We are okay."

The next thing I remember is being consoled by Jeff.

"Angie, what's wrong?"

"My babies," I wailed. "I saw my babies."

I described the dream in vivid detail. The more I talked about it, the more I cried. It felt as if they had been ripped from my arms. I wanted to go back, to see their faces again, hear their voices, and hold them.

He hugged me tightly, and I rested on his chest. I couldn't close my eyes. All I could do was envision the four of them together. I was so thankful God had given me this dream. I wholeheartedly believe they were my children. I couldn't prove it to anyone, but my heart warmed and for the first time in a long time, I felt peace.

I spent the next day trying to remember every bit of the dream, trying to burn any detail into my memory. I never wanted to forget what they looked like or what happened in the dream. It was one of the most precious gifts I had been given.

When Grace Anna awoke, I hugged her with everything in me. She probably thought I was losing my mind. I kissed every inch of her sweet chubby face.

"Mom, what are you doing?"

"I'm loving you," I said as I hugged her again.

"Okay. But I want to go play."

"I want you to know I love you, sweet girl. I always will."

"I know." She rolled into her room to play.

Grace Anna had no idea how profoundly her words about her siblings being okay would affect me. She had simply said what came from her heart. She didn't know about my struggles to forgive myself for things I had done as a young person.

It was no coincidence to me that Grace Anna knew about her siblings around the same time I had the dream. I had longed to release my shame and guilt over my first pregnancy and miscarriage. I wanted my child I lost to know I loved him and would have cherished being his momma. I also needed to know my other children were happy and safe.

The message Grace Anna and my children in the dream shared kept running through my mind—they were okay. I finally realized God had been taking care of my children in heaven. And He would continue to do so.

The dream was not merely a glimpse of my children; it was a message for me to let go and allow God to heal my heart. I had to forgive myself and those who had hurt me in the past. I could not hang onto the guilt and hurt if I wanted to be happy and fulfilled.

After that night, I let go of all the guilt and shame. I let go of punishing myself over mistakes made by a young and naïve girl. I made the decision to look forward to the days I had with my children on earth and to the day my family circle would be reunited in heaven.

Grace Anna's knowledge of her siblings remains a blessing to me. It was the catapult that sent my healing into motion, and I will cherish her words and the dream the rest of my life.

God doesn't want us to live in shame. I asked for forgiveness twenty years ago, and He gave it. But it wasn't until then that I finally forgave myself. God's love had healed my old wound, and I could finally be free.

Little did I know, only a few months down the road, our family would face a tragedy that would break our hearts and test our faith. We needed God more than ever, and Grace Anna would once again bring words to mend our hearts.

ADVOCATE IN ACTION

I have always had a tender heart for people with physical and intellectual disabilities. Often though, I feared I would say something inappropriate and hurt their feelings. After having Grace Anna, I realized they wanted to be loved and treated like everyone else—with respect.

Kyra Phillips of CNN and Headline News referred Patty Dempsey to me. Patty was a longtime advocacy leader in Kentucky. She had worked tirelessly for the Arc of Kentucky to help people with disabilities through education and leadership. Her joy and enthusiasm was contagious.

My first speaking engagement was at the Arc of Kentucky's annual conference. I was the keynote speaker, and Grace Anna would sing. I had never planned to be a keynote speaker. I was terrified of public speaking. I sweated. I cried. I wrung my hands. Inside I felt as if I was not cut out for it, but for my daughter, I would do it.

Oh Lord, send me the words.

I got up and started my speech.

As I told my story, the crowd was very attentive.

Hey, they are not throwing tomatoes at me. I might actually be half decent at this.

My hands weren't shaking, my voice wasn't cracking, and I wasn't gasping for each breath. Toward the end of the presentation, a fire welled up in me. A fire to touch others through our story. All the fear left. I realized when you speak about something you've lived, it flows. I didn't use my notes. I spoke straight from my heart. God had given me the words to say, and that is what made the difference.

Once I finished, it was Grace Anna's turn to sing. Her little body shook with excitement. And when she belted out "Amazing Grace" as if she were onstage at the Grand Ole Opry, I got goosebumps all over me. I thought it was cool that here she was, my tiny little girl, singing to a room full of people she hardly knew. It moved them to give her a standing ovation. Her testimony of love and hope rang out through her song. My speech may have touched their hearts, but her singing lifted their spirits.

After meeting many members of the audience, it was clear God had used my speech to touch hearts. What hit me most was when young people enduring tougher health situations than Grace Anna's encouraged us. Then there were the mommas who were crying and thanking us for making a difference.

It was such a humbling experience to be a part of a profoundly tough group of people—a group of people who get overlooked because they don't fit the description of normal. My Grace Anna wasn't deemed normal by doctors, and I'm sure these parents had heard some of the same lines I had. But we were a family now, and I was determined to fight for my new family, fight the right way with love, education, and advocacy.

Patty and I kept in touch monthly, and she notified me of programs and events that would address Grace Anna's needs. One thing we needed was a wheelchair-accessible bathroom.

I had been holding Grace Anna up in my arms to bathe her. It was taking a toll on my body and becoming a little embarrassing for her. By then she was much older and needed to gain independence by doing things other little girls do without their mommas, like using the bathroom.

One of the programs Patty recommended was the Hart-Supported Living Program grant. We were fortunate, after the second year of trying, to receive the grant. Many people apply year after year and are never chosen. I definitely believe God had a part in it. People from all over the world wrote letters of support to help us get the grant, which facilitated the installation of a roll-in shower, a wheelchair-accessible sink, and a toilet for a small-stature person. It was a blessing far greater than my mind could have ever imagined. We went from a tiny shower stall to an open, easy-access shower where Grace Anna could bathe herself. Each part of the bathroom focused on specific needs for Grace Anna. It seemed as if we'd been given the keys to the Taj Mahal of bathrooms.

"Momma, what in the world!" Grace Anna said when she first saw her new bathroom. "What kind of shower is this?"

"It's your shower, Peanut," I replied. "Now you can sit right here in your shower chair and take a shower on your own."

"Well, you don't have to leave yet. You can stay and talk to me, can't you?"

"Yes, ma'am. If you need my help, just ask. This is a new adventure for all of us."

I never heard of someone crying over a shower, but both of us sat in the bathroom, crying and hugging and looking at the glorious gift we had been given.

Receiving blessings like this hammered in the idea that we should pass on blessings to as many people as we could. God had been so good to us, we should share things we had learned to let them know about programs that could enable them to lead better, happier lives. We were also firm believers in giving financially to people in need and charities that help people.

This leads me to Stella. I had heard Stella sing at church many times, and I honestly was quite envious of her voice. She was confident and stylish with a powerhouse voice. But I didn't even know her name until one afternoon when I was sitting in the parking lot of a local grocery store.

There she was, walking around with a smile on her face and a bounce in her step, and she wanted to meet Grace Anna. I thought it was quite funny. I had always wanted to chat with her but could not figure out where to start, and here she was, dying to meet my sweet girl. It's funny how God works things out. He sees who needs to be put together at the right time and right place, especially when His servants are a little hesitant.

After a few selfies and small talk, we had bonded. Later I learned she worked at our local school board in the special education department, and she had a son with Williams syndrome named Clayton. A fearless advocate for people with disabilities, she was right there in my small hometown and I had never known.

A few months down the road, she messaged me: "Hey, Angie, there is a training for parents about special education coming up. I would love to see you there."

"Of course. Tell me when and where. I'll be there."

This was the first of many times she guided me through steps to be a strong advocate for Grace Anna. The best advice came when she encouraged me to get training through the Arc of Kentucky's Advocates in Action program. Little did I know that training would facilitate the opportunity to make an impression on a leader in our state.

The training gave people like me tools to utilize our strengths and build upon our weaknesses when advocating for our children. It also helped people with disabilities to be strong advocates themselves. We were encouraged to contact our local representatives about meeting with them during an upcoming event at the capitol in Frankfort called the Rally in the Rotunda. It was part of the 874K Disabilities Coalition Rally that happens each year. I was also asked to speak at the event, and Grace Anna was invited to sing. I felt the need to jump in head first and do the best possible presentation I could to help those in similar situations to ours.

I contacted my local representatives and asked for appointments. I did not receive any replies. It was discouraging. So, what did I do? Seek someone a little higher on the ladder.

I'm the type of person who believes we are all equal, so to me our governor is just like me. Someone's position, income, race, religion, or gender doesn't matter. I treat all people with respect, and I expect the same in return. To me, our government works for us, so it wouldn't be ridiculous to ask the governor for a meeting while we were at the rally.

One long email later, I hoped he would give our family a meeting, and I was overjoyed to receive the email with a time and date to meet with him. Next, I had to prioritize what I was going to say. We were slotted a fifteen-minute session, and I would take advantage of every second I could get an ear to listen.

As I stood at the front of the rotunda, my nerves were getting the best of me. Once again, I called upon the Lord to give me words to touch hearts and change minds. I felt my body relax, my mind calm, and my focus set.

My voice echoed through the large opening in the capitol. I could see everyone listening very intently, and my sweet girl was right by my side the entire time. It was as if she knew this moment was very important.

Besides a little of Grace Anna's story, the two topics I spoke about were the Michelle P. Waiver and the Hart-Supported Living Program grant. Both programs were essential for our Grace Anna to live a safe and happy life.

Grace Anna smiled dearly at me the entire time I delivered my speech. It was very soothing to see the promise in her face that everything was okay. Then it was her turn. I never tell her what to sing but always leave it up to her. And what did she choose? "Amazing Grace."

She sang like an angel. This tiny little girl in a wheelchair sang with such a strong, powerful voice. If that didn't get the attention of our leaders, I don't know what could have. What touched me the most was seeing people with disabilities delightedly cheering her on. They were being heard that day. Grace Anna was a voice for them to be heard loudly and clearly.

After such a long day, I figured Grace Anna would be exhausted when we started to our next appointment, meeting our governor. As usual, she was excited to meet someone new and turn on her charm.

Governor Matt Bevin greeted us warmly. "Good afternoon," he said, shaking our hands.

Immediately Grace Anna felt at ease with Governor Bevin, giggling and laughing with him. She felt no intimidation by his stature in our state, and he treated us as if he had known us his entire life.

I handed Governor Bevin my list of concerns and expressed how each of them were dear to our hearts. We talked about Grace Anna's life and how she influenced others. He was very empathetic toward our situation and listened to our concerns.

"She has changed our lives so much for the better," Jeff said. "These programs have really helped us make life better for Grace Anna and helped us take care of her."

"She is definitely a blessing," he replied. "Do you mind if I hold her?"

I turned to Grace Anna. "Would you like to go to Governor Bevin?"

There was no hesitation in her body. She bolted out of her wheelchair into my arms, then into Governor Bevin's arms. She hugged him tightly, laying her head upon his shoulder. With a big ol' smile plastered across her face, she cackled delightfully at everything he said. I don't know who was more mesmerized, her or him.

It was evident in the way Governor Bevin interacted with Grace Anna that he was a caring dad. Little did I know, he had nine children at home. He had also suffered the heartbreaking loss of his oldest daughter in a car accident. His love of his family struck a chord with me. Clearly, he loved children and wanted what was best for them.

Before we knew it, our fifteen-minute meeting had turned into a forty-five-minute visit. We had discussed everything from the Hart-Supported Living Program grant to our beloved Kentucky Wildcats. Even though he didn't ask, I knew he probably had things he needed to accomplish.

Upon leaving, Governor Bevin gave us a direct number to reach him if we ever needed anything for Grace Anna or had questions for him. His helpful assistant, Taylor Sears, made arrangements for us to receive photos of that day and helped us understand how to set up direct communications between the governor and us.

On a couple of occasions when we were having issues with Grace Anna's health coverage, Governor Bevin's staff helped us get in touch with people to find answers. I had struggled for months trying to get approval for a spine surgery. I worried it wasn't going to happen. Governor Bevin's team worked tirelessly to help us figure out what the holdup was and get it resolved.

We continue to stay in touch with Governor Bevin and appreciate the help he gave us. We truly believe he seeks out the best for our state. Most of my life I've not had much access to political leaders. I never felt the urgency to reach out to one until Grace Anna came along. Some people think politicians are self-absorbed and have their own agendas, but Governor Bevin was nothing like that. He seemed very genuine, especially when it came to caring for Kentucky, his family, and his faith. I don't agree with him on every issue, but I do feel if I have concerns, he will listen with an open mind and heart.

After my interactions with Governor Bevin, Stella, and Patty, I felt a push in my spirit to continue my advocacy work. I contacted parents in our local community and agencies within our state to find ways to help people with disabilities. With Stella's help, I also formed Partnership in Leadership and Advocacy Network in my home county. I conferenced with parents, guiding them to programs and organizations that could help them.

I also encouraged parents to help their children become advocates for themselves. They have a voice that needs to be heard. I can say something that affects Grace Anna over and over, only to have it fall upon deaf ears. When Grace Anna says the same thing, it opens more minds because it comes from her.

I was also very blessed to be chosen by Governor Bevin to be a part of the Hart-Supported Living Council in 2017, which is an opportunity to serve my state and have my voice heard on a program that is very dear to my heart.

Having Grace Anna not only changed the course of my life but the woman I was becoming. I had struggled my entire life with speaking in front of crowds or even a small group of my peers. But after advocating for my daughter and children like her, I felt strong when standing before others, because God had given me a message of hope. He had also touched my heart with a passion for helping people in similar situations. I relied on God to help me let go of the fear and give me the right words each time I spoke.

Life had started making sense to me. Grace Anna was improving, I had learned to be a strong advocate for her, Jeff was enjoying his work, and Isaiah was embarking on his senior year of high school. Our heartaches were easing up, but we had no idea the hardest blows waited right around the corner.

20

A TIME TO MOURN

Loss of any loved one is tremendously hard, but it seems unexpected losses shock our spirit and test our faith to the deepest level. From March 2014 through July 2016, our family faced the death of four family members. Each was an important part of our lives, but the unexpected death of one of them shook our family to its core.

My grandma Mary Belle had never spared her thoughts on matters. Sometimes she could be harsh, but you always knew what to expect. She never held back her opinions. She was also one of the tidiest and most organized humans I ever knew.

She never was the touchy-feely type, but you knew she cared about you. The last three years of her life, she battled dementia. It took a very confident, strong woman and turned her into a dependent and frightened lady. Her personality changed also. She hugged us more and told us she loved us every time we saw her. She thought Grace Anna hung the moon.

She and Grace Anna had a special relationship. She loved and hugged on Grace Anna so deeply and affectionately, it made my heart joyful.

During her last two years, she became so ill she had to be hospitalized, and it seemed wrong. She had always kept her home spotless and lived life to the fullest. In the hospital, however, she was on a strict schedule, her room was not how she liked it, her clothes were not maintained to her standards, and her choices were very limited.

The last time I saw her, I brought both Grace Anna and Isaiah with me. She sang gospel hymns with the other patients. I had never heard my grandma sing a gospel song. She sang beautifully. I had missed this part of my grandma growing up. I wondered why she had not shown it. It was an experience I will always cherish.

"Angie, I want to go home to be with Jesus and my mom," she said.

A few months later, Grandma Mary Belle got her heart's desire. She took her last breath and went to spend eternity with Jesus and her mom. Grace Anna brought out a side of Grandma Mary Belle that changed the way I remembered her.

At the time of Grandma Mary Belle's death, her daughter, my aunt Inga, was battling cancer, which made things so much more difficult for my extended family and me. Aunt Inga had defied the odds for four years. Her doctors had prepared her for the worst many times, but she fought to stay alive.

Aunt Inga was one of the most active, healthiest people I've ever known. She loved riding horses and taking care of her animals. But, as I have seen, cancer doesn't care who you are but attacks the healthiest people. Aunt Inga loved to sing karaoke, and I'm sure Grace Anna got some of her showmanship from her. Grace Anna loved to interact with Aunt Inga. Their resilience made them very close.

"There's my girl," Aunt Inga would say, always greeting Grace Anna with a hug and a smile even though I knew she was in excruciating pain.

Grace Anna would hop up right beside Aunt Inga and sing her a song. It touched Aunt Inga's heart so much. The last few weeks of her life, we visited her in the hospital and Grace Anna sang to her.

"Angie, please bring her back tomorrow," Aunt Inga requested.

It was the least I could do, knowing what she faced.

Until the cancer became too painful and her body grew too tired, Aunt Inga held on. She wanted to spend as much time with her family as she could. Looking at her beautiful face, you would never know she was sick. She always was a gorgeous woman.

We had our last conversation while Grace Anna and I visited her in the hospital. "I'm ready to go home," she said. Three days later she did.

A little over six months after Grandma Mary Belle died, Aunt Inga joined her in heaven. The loss of two strong matriarchs fell hard on my family. The glue that held us together lost its effectiveness once they passed away.

Thanksgiving and Christmas were extremely tough in 2014. The loss of Grandma Mary Belle and Aunt Inga took a toll on everyone's hearts. We just wanted to make it through the holidays and start a new year fresh. We had no idea the upcoming year would bring an unexpected death that would leave our family heartbroken.

The last time we had seen Freddie, Isaiah's dad, was Father's Day. He had dropped Isaiah off after a visit. He thanked Jeff for being so good to Isaiah. Jeff and Freddie always got along very well, something that was wonderful to me. It showed Isaiah you can move on from things in the past and work together for the good of the children and everyone's sanity.

And Freddie loved Grace Anna.

"Hey, Gracie," he said, smiling from ear to ear.

He then picked her up, kissed her cheek, and hugged her. He was the only person who called her Gracie, and she adored him. After Grace Anna was born, it healed the tension that still existed between us at times due to the divorce. Freddie loved my little girl, was friends with Jeff, and even spent Christmas at my home. We were all doing well as one big blended family.

Then the unimaginable happened.

Ring, ring, ring. Early in the morning on July 29, 2015, the phone chimed.

My mom was calling to invite all the grandchildren to a big breakfast. "You guys come over. I'm making biscuits, gravy, sausage … all your favorites. Try to be here around nine."

"We will get dressed and be on our way."

After lots of eating and conversation, we all sat around and watched some movies. It was a treat for the kids to go to Mom's to eat her cooking. She is one of the best cooks in the world. After resting a bit, we headed back home to get ready for church.

I decided I needed to work on health insurance papers instead of going to church, so Isaiah went with his girlfriend in another county. It was a very rainy night, so I advised him to be careful.

"The roads can be very slick after it's been dry so long. Watch what you're doing," I advised. "And don't forget to ask your dad for his address. We need it for your health insurance."

"I know, Mom, I know."

A few hours later, Isaiah texted me to let me know he was on his way home. "Dad hasn't gotten back to me with the address yet. I'll try him again."

His relationship with his dad had been strained the past couple of months due to a disagreement in the family. As with all families, we had disagreements at times. It doesn't mean you stop loving each other. It just means everyone is human. Things get worked out in time, and we move past those disagreements—if there is enough time left to work it out, that is.

Another hour went by.

I started to worry where Isaiah was, so I tried calling him again. No answer.

Fifteen minutes later, the home phone rang. Isaiah was so frantic I couldn't understand a word he said except *Mom*.

"Isaiah, calm down, honey. Take some breaths."

"Mom, Dad has been in a wreck. Mom, please."

"Is someone with you?"

"Yes, Shawn is."

At the time Isaiah was dating the daughter of a state trooper, who took the phone and tried to explain what was going on. "Angie, this is Shawn. Freddie was in a car accident. He didn't make it."

"No!" I screamed. "That can't be true." I fell to the floor, dropped the phone, and began sobbing.

Jeff picked up the phone and got Isaiah's location from Shawn.

We loaded into the car to go meet him. I felt numb, as if it were all a dream. I dreaded seeing Isaiah's face. He loved his dad so much. I didn't know if he could handle such a tragic loss so young.

I prayed for Isaiah. *God, please wrap your arms around him. Give him your peace, the comfort only you can give.*

When we arrived, a long line of cars waited on Highway 127. I could see the flashing blue lights ahead. We turned left where Isaiah waited at a local dairy dip with Shawn and his girlfriend, Autum.

As we pulled in, Isaiah ran to us, screaming, "Mom! He's gone. He's gone." He collapsed into my arms, shaking uncontrollably and sobbing.

Jeff wrapped his arm underneath Isaiah's shoulders and helped walk him to the car. I had never heard my son in such an uncontrolled, panicky state. As his mom, I felt completely overwhelmed and unsure of what to do next.

My brother-in-law, Jamie, arrived with my sister, niece, and nephew. Jamie would drive Isaiah's car home. Isaiah was in no shape to drive. Isaiah and I sat in my car, along with his girlfriend, while Jeff discussed things with Shawn and Jamie.

Several minutes later, Jeff entered the car. "He can't see him."

Isaiah had wanted to go to the wreck and see his dad one last time, but Shawn explained to Jeff that Isaiah didn't need to see Freddie in that condition. Jeff started the car and drove us home.

Once we arrived home, Jamie, Bobbie, Myla, and Nate waited for us on our front porch. They surrounded Isaiah in one gigantic hug. Bellows of sorrow filled the air. The combination of grief and shock overtook our reality. I wrapped my arms around them and wept profusely.

We finally moved inside our home. We all sat in the living room, questioning what had happened. How was this possible?

"Mom," Isaiah said through tears, "he just sent me a text saying, 'Come see me, Son,' and that he loved me. He can't be gone."

"Isaiah," I tried to reply.

"I sent him the text that I loved him. He had to get it. I know he did."

I tried to comfort him. "Son, your dad knew you loved him. It doesn't matter what happened last week, last month, last year. He knew you loved him, and he loved you more than anyone on this earth."

I finally convinced him to try to go to bed a little after midnight. He didn't rest much though. I heard him get up and down through the night. And I heard his sobbing. I wanted to take his pain away, but I knew this was a pain only God and time could heal.

The next morning, it still seemed like a dream. Isaiah had many questions about why it happened, but we couldn't find any answers. Even if we had found the answers, I don't think it would have made him feel any better.

Our pastor, Brother Hershel, stopped by and talked with Isaiah on the porch swing. I don't know exactly what was said, but when Isaiah returned, he was calmer than he had been before.

"I'm so glad he stopped by, Mom," he said. "We had a good talk."

I knew the next few days would be very difficult for him. He would help choose the casket, the music, and other aspects of the funeral.

"Mom, will you go with me?" he asked.

"Of course, Son. Let me know what you want me to do."

After a meeting at the funeral home, everything was in place for the funeral. The service represented Freddie to a T. He would have loved the music and the arrangements. Isaiah even picked the hat Freddie wore in the casket. Isaiah seemed to handle it all so well, maybe too well.

One day after Isaiah buried his dad, he started his senior year in high school. I tried to get him to stay at home for a while, but he refused. Weeks went by, and he wouldn't speak of Freddie. He held everything in and avoided mentioning anything associated with his dad. I worried he would slide into depression if he didn't talk openly about how he felt.

"Isaiah, it's okay if you talk about your dad. It helps if you talk to someone about things on your mind."

"Mom, I just worry. Was he ready?"

Grace Anna was sitting on my lap, listening to the entire conversation. She never interrupted or made a sound until we finished discussing things.

"Mom," Grace Anna said, "don't you know? Freddie is in heaven with my sisters and Aunt Inga. I saw them. They are happy. Freddie was running with my sisters. He's with them."

Both Isaiah and I wept. Neither one of us could get a word out.

"Don't be sad. Be happy. He's taking care of them," Grace Anna added.

Isaiah moved to sit beside us on the couch and hugged Grace Anna and me. Tears streamed down his face.

Grace Anna wiped away his tears. "It's going to be okay, Bubba."

Then Isaiah smiled.

It wasn't the end of the grieving process, but it was a start of better days. He began talking about his dad and remembering the good times they had together. He laughed again and facing the day got easier.

One would think our family had experienced enough grief in such a short amount of time, but that wouldn't be the case.

I had always been very close to Grandma Elma. Some of my best childhood memories are from when I would spend the week with her, helping her can vegetables, wash clothes, and do other chores around the house.

Grandma Elma called my house almost every day. If we weren't home, she would leave very long messages describing her day and expressing her love for us. In her last message, she made sure we knew she loved us, as if she knew she were getting closer to death.

"Angie, it's Grandma. Where is my great, big, beautiful doll, Grace Anna? I love you all. You're going to have to get over here and help me fix my hair. I sure do miss you all. You know I love you and love to hear my girl sing. I'll talk to you later. Call me when you get home. I wish you and Grace Anna could stay here with me. I love you all so much."

My beloved Grandma Elma had been battling health problems for many years. She had almost died in flight to a hospital after complications during heart surgery, but she lived to tell about the remarkable experience of being shocked back to life. Each time life had thrown her a curve ball, she had fought her way back. Grace Anna gets some of her toughness from her.

This time she had a tumor in her breast, and Grandma wouldn't allow doctors to treat it. Deep down, I think she feared chemo or radiation. She didn't want to leave this world as some of her family had after suffering through cancer treatments. She fought it for months but ended up needing hospice treatment in a local hospital.

The night before she died, Grace Anna, Isaiah, and I traveled to the hospital to visit her. Grace Anna rolled over and said, "Grandma, I'm here."

Grandma Elma was unresponsive. Grace Anna began singing "Amazing Grace" and Grandma murmured a few sounds, but nothing we could make out. Grace Anna and I sat down beside her, leaned over, and kissed her cheek. "I love you," we both said.

Grandma Elma tried her best to respond, moving her mouth. The words wouldn't come out, but I knew she was saying I love you.

My heart ached to see such a tough lady be ravaged by cancer. In early morning, July 9, 2016, Grandma Elma took her last breath. Her pain and suffering were over, but her absence left a hole in my heart. Grace Anna had the honor of singing "Amazing Grace" and "What a Day That Will Be" at her funeral three days later.

Our family had been through a horrendous period of loss the last few years, and we were ready for better days. We had experienced a season of weeping and mourning. Now we needed a time for laughing and dancing. The four deaths had left gaping hollows in our daily lives, but with everything in life, we had to find a way to move on.

God will always comfort and guide, if we ask. I knew refocusing our lives on the positive things, not just the negatives, would lighten our spirits. Even though death was not what we wanted for our family members, it could be the ultimate healing from pain and agony. Our family members were not in pain anymore, and we needed to respect their lives by cherishing each moment.

Grace Anna had been connected to each of them in her own unique way. Her sweet spirit brought out wonderful attributes in them, some I had never seen. She also helped mend the pain a divorce can leave between people. God used her pure spirit to enhance their lights. We were blessed to know them all and will never forget their impact on our lives.

During all the losses we had faced, Grace Anna's health had remained moderately well. No major issues caused concern. She was ready for a rod extension at the hospital, so we prepared for her upcoming surgery. But as life would have it, we had another mountain to climb before anything could be done about her back. A series of situations arose that would not only test my patience with hospitals and doctors but push me to be an even bolder advocate for Grace Anna.

21

THE BEST-LAID PLANS

It's funny how we always think we have things figured out. I planned for Grace Anna to go to the same hospital for treatment for as long as she was on this earth. The doctors were awesome, and she did so well. I couldn't think of anything that would change that.

Then I made the choice to take a medical leave to provide care for her after her rod insertion. When I did this, I didn't realize how the change from an employer-provided insurance to Kentucky Medicaid would influence my daughter's health care.

Grace Anna had been a patient of her doctor for over three years. We were comfortable with him and confident in his abilities to help her medically. He had successfully performed a spinal fusion when she was eighteen months old, and placed a lengthening rod in her spine when she was four that had worked amazingly.

After an appointment in the fall of 2014, a rod lengthening was scheduled for February 2015. Two weeks prior to surgery, I called the doctor's office to see if she needed blood work or anything else done before the surgery.

"We are having an issue with your insurance," the receptionist said.

"What do you mean? She has surgery in two weeks. What is the problem?"

"The hospital will not accept Kentucky Medicaid. You can fill out some forms, but I'm not positive it will help."

That was the first I had heard of the problem. I was enraged. What were we going to do? The rod in her back had to be lengthened. As soon as we hung up, I dialed the main line to the doctor's assistant.

"This is ridiculous," I said. "How can they not take Medicaid?"

"It is out of our hands. There is no agreement between Kentucky Medicaid and the hospital, so they will not allow us to do the surgery."

Being the hardhead I am, I wouldn't take her answer as the end of the discussion. I demanded a conversation with Grace Anna's doctor. The next morning, he called our home. He had discussed things with the administration, and they still would not budge. I was amazed that a top health-care institution could turn its back on a patient and not even try to work with Kentucky Medicaid.

After phone calls with Kentucky Medicaid, I soon came to realize I would be wasting my time if I continued fighting for Grace Anna to remain a patient at that hospital. For whatever reason, an agreement could not be made to cover her procedure.

I could have allowed my emotions to get the best of me. I wasn't happy with the hospital administration, but fighting with them wasn't getting us any closer to Grace Anna's rod being lengthened. I decided to let it go and move on.

The search began to find a new doctor with experience and expertise in treating spinal issues in children with Conradi-Hünermann syndrome. The old saying, "finding a needle in a haystack," was an understatement. It is extremely difficult to find experienced doctors to treat children with rare disorders. It felt as if I was at the bottom of the ocean, blindly looking for a glimpse of light to help me swim my way out. The search was not easy.

A month had passed from when Grace Anna's rod should have been lengthened. Jeff and I frantically searched for someone capable of providing Grace Anna with excellent, not just adequate, care. We met with Dr. Talwalkar, who had previously treated Grace Anna at Shriner's Hospital, but after praying about it, we didn't feel comfortable returning to Shriner's.

It wasn't anything we didn't like about the hospital or Dr. Tal-walkar, whom we had always loved. It was the amount of experience he had with children with Conradi-Hünermann syndrome, which was not extensive.

After a month of research, I found no doctors in Kentucky with ample experience in treating patients with Conradi, so we looked elsewhere. Many of the families in our support group went to the Texas Scottish Rite Hospital for Children, but due to the great distance, we kept searching.

"What are we going to do? The rod needs lengthened," I told Jeff. "If we keep waiting, it could cause irreversible damage to her spine."

"We will find someone," he replied. "Just keep calling and looking. Someone we can put our trust in will pop up."

I wish I believed him, but I doubted we would find someone as experienced as Dr. Ain.

Then one day I came upon an article about patients with Conradi being treated by a Dr. Peter Sturm. The doctor had been associated with Conradi patients, but I couldn't get full access to the article.

Where is this doctor?

To my surprise, he was at Cincinnati Children's Hospital.

Why hadn't we known about him before? Grace Anna had already seen five doctors there. How was it possible we had never heard about Dr. Sturm before? I didn't waste any time over-analyzing the situation. I got off the computer and on the phone. Within moments Grace Anna had an appointment for a consultation with Dr. Sturm. I didn't know his level of experience, but at least he had worked with Conradi patients. We hadn't come across another orthopedic surgeon who had.

The two weeks until the appointment slowly dragged on. Grace Anna's spine was curving out more than ever. I spent many nights rubbing her legs due to the pain radiating from her spine down through the nerves in her legs.

"Mom, please take the rod out. It hurts."

It was hard enough to look at her misshapen spine protruding from her back, but to hear her cry in pain ripped my insides in two. I couldn't let her see it was grieving me tremendously. If I broke down, she would become afraid and even more upset.

I sat up in bed, then placed her upon my shoulder, rubbing the back of her legs. I would sing and sing until she fell asleep, then place her on her belly to sleep. Looking at her, I thought of how unfair it was that a sweet spirit like her would have to live through the pain every night. When most people see her joyful face on social media, they see the person she wants others to see. Only Jeff, Isaiah, and I saw how she struggled each day, enduring pain most adults couldn't handle.

She didn't want people to know she hurt. It embarrassed her if others pitied her. Grace Anna had always proven to be one of the strongest human beings I've ever met. She never allowed the pain to rob her of her joy; rather, she chose to be happy when it seemed like there was no reason.

Finally, the day arrived, and we were on our way to Cincinnati. Jeff and I hoped we would return home with a new orthopedic surgeon for Grace Anna.

Within moments of arriving, we were placed in a patient room. A nurse entered and interviewed us, asking all the important questions about Grace Anna's previous spine issues.

What surgeries had Grace Anna had? Did she have any issues with surgeries? Did she have any other health concerns? Did she complain of pain?

It seemed as if we answered a million questions, which made us feel confident they were competent. We'd come to learn that if a doctor and his staff don't ask many questions, they are probably not the ones to treat our daughter.

"Thank you all so much. Dr. Sturm will be in shortly," the nurse said as she exited the room.

"Well, I think this is going to work out," Jeff said.

"I know. They are very thorough," I added. "I hope the doctor is as wonderful as the nurse was."

After a few minutes, Dr. Sturm entered the room, introduced himself, and shook our hands. He was a very friendly man, and I was grateful for his pleasant demeanor. Lately, Grace Anna had become anxious when meeting new doctors, this one seemed to be a good fit for her.

After a few questions about Grace Anna's spinal surgery history, Jeff was ready to grill him. "Have you worked with kids with Conradi-Hünermann much?"

I almost snickered. Since not many people had Conradi, I wondered how he would answer.

"I actually did a study with colleagues to help with the spinal treatment and research of seventeen patients with chondrodysplasia punctata. A large percentage of these patients had the specific form, Conradi-Hünermann syndrome, that Grace Anna has."

In all the years I had been interacting with doctors since Grace Anna was born, I had never met a doctor with the level of experience that he had in treating people with Conradi-Hünermann syndrome. We were shocked that neither one of us had ever heard of him. We had combed the Internet since she was born, seeking doctors with that same expertise.

As we talked through Grace Anna's X-rays and medical reports, it was apparent she needed her rod lengthened as soon as possible. He also suggested seeing another doctor in his group, Dr. James McCarthy, to help with Grace Anna's leg and hip issues.

After meeting with Dr. Sturm, we were confident he was the doctor to take over Grace Anna's spinal care. A huge boulder had been lifted from my chest. I could breathe easier and relax a little more knowing she was well cared for.

After returning home, I called Cincinnati Children's to speak with Dr. McCarthy about Grace Anna's leg issues. He ordered a gait analysis lab at Cincinnati Children's Physical Therapy Department to get the tests performed.

Within a month we were in Cincinnati again to see what they could find with the gait analysis. The physical therapists placed stickers on her legs, hips, and back to read nerve impulses being relayed throughout her body. Her physical therapist, Joanna, was concerned all the muscles in her legs were not firing.

With assistance Grace Anna walked the length of the testing facility many times as the information was recorded. When the results were analyzed, it gave wonderful news: all muscles were firing. She should be able to build her leg and core strength, enabling her to one day walk—maybe not like everyone else, but at least there was hope she'd be able to walk her own way.

For some time, we had been concerned about Grace Anna's left leg. She had a severe contracture in the hip and a dislocated knee cap that prevented her from walking. Since the nerve conductivity test showed nerve impulses were being delivered and the muscles were firing, we figured the contracture and knee cap were the main reasons she wasn't walking.

The next week we had our initial appointment with Dr. McCarthy and our second appointment with Dr. Sturm.

When Dr. McCarthy, with his friendly personality, entered the room, he and Grace Anna hit it off very quickly. She loved joking around with him. It always helps when doctors have a good bedside manner, especially with children.

"Upon looking at her X-rays taken today, I see her knee is dislocated. But we have a bigger problem. Her right hip is dislocated," Dr. McCarthy explained. "I feel we need to do an exam under anesthesia when her rod is lengthened to see if I can get it to go back in and stay in."

This news stunned Jeff and me. Grace Anna had not complained at all about any pain or problems with her left leg. I felt like the most horrible mother on the planet. Why hadn't I noticed? How could I have missed her hip being dislocated?

"Dr. McCarthy, how is this possible? She hasn't cried or complained about the hip."

"It's hard to say. Grace Anna more than likely deals with pain every day. To her it may not seem horrible."

Even though he was trying to comfort us, I still felt awful. I struggled with the thoughts of Grace Anna being in pain daily. How could I help her? Could I have paid more attention to how she moved or reacted? Whatever the reason, I had to let it go and focus on getting her better. Beating myself up was not going to help her.

After a visit with Dr. Sturm, we were scheduled for a procedure to lengthen the rod, evaluate the hip, and insert an ear tube—all in one day in late spring. Grace Anna struggled with anesthesia at times, so we strove to accomplish as much as possible during one sedation.

Due to some miscommunication between doctors, however, things did not go as planned. Once Dr. Sturm was in the operating room, an assistant with the rod company was not positive they had the right equipment to lengthen the rod. Once again, the rod lengthening was postponed.

"I don't feel comfortable opening her up if it is the wrong equipment," Dr. Sturm explained.

"I understand, but where does this put us on lengthening the rod?" I asked.

"She's safe for right now. We will contact the previous surgeon and make sure of the equipment in her back. As long as we get it lengthened in three to four months, she will be fine," he assured us.

Her dislocated hip was another story. Only surgery would fix it. Upon examination, however, doctors determined that Grace Anna's hip would not stay in once it was placed back in the hip socket. This meant she would have to have surgery to build the hip and socket up. Plus, she'd be in a cast for eight to ten weeks.

That wasn't what we were hoping to hear.

After many phone calls and a few visits to Cincinnati, we were once again scheduled for rod lengthening, along with a hip surgery, at the end of August.

Grace Anna had already been through so much in her young life; the thought of another big surgery was disheartening. I wondered if the hip had been out for a while, and why hadn't her previous doctors noticed it? Most likely I will never get an answer to those questions.

We had planned for Grace Anna to keep the same orthopedic surgeon her entire childhood, but life does not always go as we planned. Maybe these doctors would be better for Grace Anna. Only time would tell if that was true.

August arrived and not only was she scheduled to have her rod lengthened but she now had to have a hip repaired from being out of socket. This added time and repositioning in the operating room. We were nervous but ready for Grace Anna to make it through her first surgery on her spine at Cincinnati Children's Hospital.

Procedures at Cincinnati were quite different than the previous hospital. To keep the room sterile, we were not permitted to enter the surgery room with Grace Anna. There was also a change in who would be doing the surgeries.

Originally Dr. Sturm would operate on her back and Dr. McCarthy would operate on her hip. Dr. Sturm was injured in an accident, so Dr. McCarthy would do both procedures. We were very confident in his abilities; he was the head of the department after all.

After we walked away from the operating room door, I could hear her calling for me, "Momma, Momma."

It shattered my nerves. *Oh Lord, please be with her.*

The next three hours seemed like an eternity.

Melissa Jarboe flew in from Kansas to support us through the surgery.

"Okay, let's work on this website," she said, trying to keep my mind off the surgery.

"All right, let's do it."

For the next two hours, she stayed by my side, never allowing me to think about what could go wrong during the surgery. Before we knew it, Dr. McCarthy paged us to meet with him.

"Everything went very well," he said. "We inserted a supportive piece that will need to be removed within a year. The cast will come off in eight weeks, and the rod also lengthened without any complications. You should be able to see her in ICU in a few moments."

He went over some postoperative care instructions with the cast and made sure we knew he and his colleagues would be in to see her each day.

When we first saw her in ICU, she looked pitiful. The cast went from halfway up her back down both legs. She couldn't move side to side, and she looked very pale.

"Momma," she began.

I rushed to her side, expecting her to cry.

"My tooth is gone, Mom. They pulled my tooth." Sure enough, her first tooth was pulled during a surgery for her hip and back.

Jeff and I took turns sitting up with her through the night. By the next morning, she was ready to move out of ICU to a floor room. Once in her new room, I had to lie in bed with her, which was fine by me. I wanted to soothe her pain the best I could, even if it was just singing to her as I held her hand.

Two days later, Grace Anna was released to go home. The new cast meant a new way to travel—strapped down to the back seat on her back. She enjoyed it. The cast also meant life at home would be different now.

We invested in a large bean bag and lots of cushiony pillows, but nothing really soothed her itching and stiffness. The powerless feeling of watching her suffer through it was extremely hard. Singing, playing games—I tried everything to keep her happy.

"I want this cast off. It hurts my back," she said, with the saddest look on her face.

"It will be over before you know it. Hang in there, honey. I'll try my best to make it better."

The weeks slowly drifted by. I checked her cast every day to make sure nothing was rubbing her or cutting off her circulation. Still, she complained about it hurting her back. I longed for the day the cast would be removed.

Finally, the day arrived for cast removal, and we all were excited.

"It's cast day!" I cheered.

Grace Anna joined in. "Woo-hoo, let's go!"

Once the cast was removed, it was easy to see why Grace Anna had been complaining of her back hurting. The cast had been rubbing her lower back the entire time, creating a pressure spot. It looked horrible and presented a new hurdle for her. She couldn't go anywhere that could lead to infection until it healed. That meant more time at home away from other people and less fun for Grace Anna.

The four weeks it took for the pressure spot to heal was not easy. It was the holidays and we wanted to see all the sites.

"Let's go see the lights, Mom," she suggested. "It would be so fun."

"I know, honey. Let's give it one more week, and if the doctors say it's okay, we will go."

After her follow-up appointment the next week, she was released to do therapy and go back into the world. Thank the Lord! She was stir-crazy, and so were the rest of us. The first thing we did was head to the Christmas lights, then to her favorite restaurant, Texas Roadhouse, for a house salad and a steak.

It wasn't the stress-free recovery we had prayed for, but Grace Anna's hip and back were in amazing shape compared to how they looked prior to surgery. The transition from the hospital to Cincinnati Children's was successful, and now we didn't have to travel so far away from home for quality healthcare.

For now, I trusted Dr. Sturm and Dr. McCarthy to make her life better and take care of her health needs. Dr. McCarthy had done an incredible job helping her hip and extending her rod. He was also very informative and caring with Grace Anna. I don't believe these doctors just magically appeared one day. God sent them to us, and we had to trust Him. It was hard for me to let go, but they had the right experience, confidence, and thoroughness in everything they did with her. I had to believe Grace Anna was receiving the best care possible.

We prayed Grace Anna's hardware would withstand the typical activities of a six-year-old girl. We had been warned if the screws in her back ever came loose, a large, dangerous surgery would have to be performed. With all our worry, Grace Anna chose to pray, pray for her heart's desire.

During all the time between surgeries, our family needed something we all could enjoy together, something fun and exciting that Grace Anna would love to do. What we came up with not only brought comfort, joy, and excitement to our lives but showed us how wonderful small towns can be for a little girl facing so much adversity. Play ball!

22

IT'S THE SMALL THINGS

The last seven years had been filled with exciting and terrifying events. We faced the heartache of miscarriage and the miracle of Grace Anna. We lost family members unexpectedly and gained new friends who enriched our lives tremendously. Grace Anna had been a constant reminder of what truly is important.

Her ability to connect with people was apparent to everyone, but many times the small things in life, like birthdays and sleepovers, didn't include friends her age. It broke my heart—and hers—that she was never invited to parties or sleepovers.

I don't believe anyone intentionally left her out. I don't think they knew how to approach it. She missed so much school due to illnesses and hospital stays that she never connected to many friends. We had no small children besides her in our family. The only close friends she had were Ava and Addie, who lived many states away.

God, she needs friends. She needs to have little-kid experiences, I prayed. *Send her someone she can play with, laugh with, and be a little girl with.*

We tried to introduce Grace Anna to children in church. I knew she would hit it off if she would go to some activities, but she still struggled with being away from me, especially if she didn't know the people very well.

"Hey, sometime maybe Grace Anna can come over and play with the girls," Shane said. "We would love to have her."

We met Shane and Amy at a small church we attended. They both were such warm, friendly people who also had three amazing children. Their two girls were around Grace Anna's age and their son was a little older.

"It would be so good for her, if she would just go," I explained. "She won't hardly leave my side."

"Well, maybe the girls could start out at your house, and then once she is comfortable, she could come to our house."

A wonderful idea.

Later that week the two girls, Payton and Addie, stood outside knocking on the door. Payton, the older of the sisters, was a gentle soul with a tender spirit. She entered the house with a gigantic smile and a hug for Grace Anna. Addie was a little shy meeting us. She stood by Payton with her arms folded together. I couldn't get her to make a peep.

"Momma, I have friends now," Grace Anna proclaimed.

I wanted to cry, but I smiled. "That's right, and they can come over whenever their parents will let them."

I was homeschooling Grace Anna due to her many surgeries and weakened immune system. She was part of a small homeschool group, but it only met a few times a year. Payton and Addie now gave Grace Anna the ability to interact with her peers.

"Ohhhhhh!" Grace Anna yelled as she whirled her wheelchair around the corner of the living room. Running close behind her were Payton and Addie, all of them cackling at the top of their lungs. The girls were fast friends. I loved how she played with them. They treated her like any other girl—I loved that even more. They never once focused on her inability to walk.

As Grace Anna flew through the doorway, I eyed Payton making sure Grace Anna wouldn't spill over onto the floor. Her caring spirit did it automatically. I don't even think she realized she was looking out for Grace Anna.

Little girls' laughter filled our home. It was heavenly. Grace Anna had never been so happy. The only problem was they had to go home eventually, and she didn't take that very well.

She shed tears and grabbed doors, which thrilled me. She acted like any other kid.

Payton and Addie came over at least once a week. Sometimes their big brother, Brayden, even joined them. He was a sports player. He loved watching the Reds with me. Like Payton, he was very protective of Grace Anna, but he did it in a way that allowed Grace Anna to be one of them, not the kid they were taking care of.

Thank you, Lord. I could not have picked better children for Grace Anna to get close to. They are wonderful.

Shane and his wife, Amy, along with their beautiful children, were now part of our lives, and I hope they remain in our lives as long as we are on this earth. Their godly hearts helped them raise three amazing children who have changed Grace Anna's life for the better.

Over the course of Grace Anna's life, our family had also changed dramatically. Our friends before Grace Anna were much different than the friends we had after her arrival. Outside of my sister and her family, our circle of friends did not live extremely close to us.

It wasn't that we didn't love our old friends. Our lives had just veered in different directions. People living similar lives became our confidants. When things got rocky, I turned to friends we made along Grace Anna's journey, like Nicole and Melissa.

At work, Jeff sought out people who would pray for and support our family. What a blessing it was for him to connect with these folks.

Life was different for us after Grace Anna was born. We called it our new normal, the normal that comes with changing your life completely to help someone in your family. It was not what we expected, but it was better than we ever could have planned. Grace Anna coming into our lives helped us finally realize that the little things, like making each other laugh or eating supper together, matter most. If everyone was healthy and happy, our life together was good.

In the meantime, Grace Anna continued to sing songs she loved. One of her favorites was a Charlie Puth song entitled "One Call Away." In it Puth tells his loved one that he will remain strong even when she is weak, and when she feels hopeless, he will be ready to comfort her. The song held a very special place in my heart. When it came out, I would sing it with Grace Anna at bedtime.

When we posted it to her Facebook, once again I never thought it would grab the attention of so many. We had sung it so much to each other it had become part of our day. I just loved it.

After 200,000 shares, it was clear the world had responded to it. By far, what most people thought was adorable was her shushing me. Grace Anna loves to perform and didn't feel she needed Momma's help that day. Her independent spirit continued to grow through her performances.

When Grace Anna started singing at our church, I was right by her side. Now I sat in the pew to the side as she sang on her own from her wheelchair. Her independence was growing, but watching her sing on her own made me ache for the days when Momma was the superhero. My girl was growing up.

Early in 2017, I signed Grace Anna up for piano lessons with Jennifer. Jennifer had taught Isaiah piano, and she taught her students to play the piano by note and by ear. Grace Anna could already play many songs by picking them out by ear. I knew Jennifer would have the personality and ability to guide her playing. Having some time away from me would also help Grace Anna gain more independence.

"Momma, listen to this."

She cheerfully played a song on her keyboard. It was like watching magic. Her body trembled as she moved her fingers across the keys. Her body swayed back and forth to the beat of the song.

"And this one."

This was a song I had never heard; the chords and melody were beautiful.

"Where did you learn that?"

"I made it up." Grace Anna grinned. "It's my heart song: *Jesus lives in my heart. He is by my side. We can all be happy when He's in our lives.*"

Her talent amazed me, but her pure spirit spoke to me more. Grace Anna never filtered things that entered her mind. She said what she felt and didn't aim to be a people pleaser. If she liked someone, it was genuine. If she didn't, it was apparent. I've only met a few people my daughter did not like being around, which made me think she felt something from them that I couldn't.

Her piano lessons helped her grow as a musician but also helped build confidence to do things on her own. Simple piano lessons were a big thing for her.

Grace Anna's improving health also enabled us to take a long-awaited vacation to Gulf Shores, thanks to our sweet friend Deana giving us a week in her condominium. The ocean was a warm escape from life at home. No doctors, no therapy, no house to clean. We could just relax and enjoy the sun and sand.

The wonder in Grace Anna's eyes as she stared out at the ocean reminded me of the wonder I felt as I looked at her at times. I was so fortunate to be her momma. I had morphed into a different woman since her birth. I went from being terrified to talk in a crowd to giving presentations to thousands of people at a time. Without Grace Anna, I never would have accomplished it. Being her mom made me stronger, bolder, and more confident in my abilities to lead others.

A family member once told me I was brave for carrying out my pregnancy. I wasn't brave. I was terrified I couldn't be the mom she needed. But over the years, I've realized God trusted me to take care of Grace Anna not only because He loves her—He loves me.

Jeff also grew as a person. He became a gentler, more compassionate man, not afraid to show the way he cared for others or his brokenness when Grace Anna tackled difficult health battles. He could be strong for her but also a teddy bear when she needed to be soothed. Grace Anna helped Jeff realize that life isn't about his desires; it's about serving others.

Isaiah's answered prayer of a sibling had come true. Grace Anna lit up his world. The closeness they developed was a beauty to see. Grace Anna challenged him with the vigor only little sisters have.

"Grace Anna, why are you running over my toe?" Isaiah asked.

"Because you're my brother."

"Stop it, turkey." And he chased her across the room.

They had the same squabbles all siblings have. The thirteen years apart and her disabilities didn't stop them from acting like your average siblings. I liked seeing them bicker. Isaiah didn't treat her extra carefully because she was in a wheelchair. She needed to know everyone in the family was important and that she was tough, capable of taking care of herself.

Grace Anna fully believed in the power of prayer. After her last surgery, she began having vivid nightmares, waking up crying out for me, and I would try to calm her.

"It's all right, honey. I'm here. You're okay."

As I tried to comfort her, she acted as if she were still in the dream. "It's trying to get my toes." So I carried her to the rocking chair and held her in my lap, singing her back to sleep.

The next night as we gathered for our nightly prayer together, Grace Anna made a special request. "Momma, please pray for my dreams."

"Of course, darling."

Each night I prayed a specific prayer for her dreams, and I made it something she could remember easily.

Lord, bless our dreams with love and grace; wake us in the morning with smiles on our faces.

She listened for it each time we prayed. If I hadn't said it, she reminded me.

Once we started praying for her dreams, the nightmares rarely occurred. She wholeheartedly believed that prayer was the reason they stopped. Her strong belief in prayer helped Grace Anna trust her biggest prayer request would come true.

For over a year, Grace Anna prayed each night for the rod in her back to be removed. We prayed over her back every night. Her heart's desire was to have a back free of hardware pushing against her skin.

Grace Anna continually kicked her legs at night until she fell asleep with her head across my chest. I knew she was uncomfortable. The only thing I could think to do was sing quietly, rub the sides of her back and legs, and pray for God to touch her.

A visit with Dr. Sturm awaited us right around the corner. We anticipated another good checkup and looked forward to scheduling her next rod lengthening.

No such luck. The screws in Grace Anna's back had worked loose.

Dr. Sturm had explained in earlier visits that if the hardware came loose, she would have to have it replaced—a very lengthy and dangerous surgery.

Jeff and I waited for the bad news. I wanted to get up and leave the room. She had been through enough. I couldn't stand to tell her she would once again spend a very long time cooped up at home, recovering from another surgery.

"Grace Anna's screws anchoring the rod have shifted out," Dr. Sturm explained. "As I look at her X-rays, her back has not gotten any worse. The rod has basically been doing nothing but lie there. The spine appears stable. I would like to go in and remove her hardware and sew her back up."

I looked at him as if he were crazy. I was so stunned I couldn't speak. Surely, I had misunderstood.

"You're saying she's not going to have anything in her back?" Jeff questioned.

"Yes."

"I'm trying to process this," I said. "I thought everything would have to be redone."

"It may have to in the future, but I would like to wait till Grace Anna is bigger and stronger. Right now, her back is holding its own. We can monitor her, and if things change, we will address that then."

"What about a brace?"

"She can wear a brace for protection."

It took a few moments to sink in. Grace Anna would be free from the rod.

Oh, that little girl prayed. She prayed for this.

Once home we discussed her upcoming surgery. "Grace Anna, Dr. Sturm is going to take the rod and all the hardware out of your back during the surgery. You may have to wear a brace, but the rod will be gone," I explained.

"Will I still get sedated?" She hated sedation during surgeries more than anything.

"Yes, and there will be a recovery time. Dr. Sturm said once you're healed up, you can even go swimming again."

Little kids aren't supposed to be excited about surgery, but Grace Anna was. "Yes!" she exclaimed. "I'm so happy, Mommy! No more rod! Woo-hoo!" I had never seen her so exhilarated in all her young life.

Jeff, on the other hand, was crushed his daughter had to look forward to a surgery. "Honey, it makes me feel awful that she is looking forward to a surgery. How is it fair a kid her age has to do the things she has to do?"

"This is a good thing. She is going to be fine. She's happy because she gets what she has wanted for a long time, no rod."

A few weeks later, I scheduled a surgery date of July 21, two days after Grace Anna's seventh birthday. Not only would we have a birthday party—we would have a miracle party.

"Life is what you make of it." I've heard that so many times since Grace Anna was born. Sometimes I wanted to tell people to stop saying it. It's easy to say stuff like that when you are not going through the same things Grace Anna had to endure, but that is exactly what Grace Anna did. She made the most of the life God gave her.

She found joy in the little things, which impressed upon our family to do the same. Life can get the best of you, if you let it. God gives each of us a divine purpose. The longer we focus on negativity, the longer until we head down the right path.

Grace Anna got her miracle, just as she had been our miracle, healing the pain of miscarriages, broken hearts, and unforeseen deaths. She became a light for the world through her resilient spirit, love of life, musical talent, and joyous personality. No, she wasn't what some doctors considered worthy of life, but oh, what a life she lived, proving to those doctors that *every* life has a purpose.

First Peter 4:10 says, "As every man hath received the gift, even so minister the same one to another, as good stewards of the manifold grace of God."

Our gift from God ministered to millions as His light burned brightly within her. Grace Anna's life is a beacon of love for everyone; her love for all people, her ability to find joy in every moment, and her tenacity to live abundantly no matter what is thrown at her, proves life truly is what you make of it. Live every second to the fullest, let your light shine—just like Grace Anna.

HOPE
FOR THE ROAD

On her seventh birthday, Grace Anna had her miracle party full of balloons, cake, a new kitten, and a group of people who loved her dearly. The love poured out for Grace Anna and the joy that filled her heart overflowed throughout the room. God blessed us with such amazing people in our lives who deeply cared for Grace Anna and our family. We hope you have some miracle parties of your own.

On August 21, 2017, Grace Anna received her miracle. Doctors removed all hardware from her spine and hip. The morning after the surgery, she looked at me from her hospital bed and said, "Momma, I feel so much better. I don't hurt, and I don't have a rod in my back anymore." The empathy and level of care shown by Dr. Sturm and Dr. McCarthy, along with all of the Cincinnati Children's Hospital staff, was incredible. It is such an amazing facility.

In the next few months, Grace Anna will begin an intensive physical therapy program and be one step closer to standing and walking on her own. I truly believe one day I will see my daughter walk.

As for the rod, doctors have advised us that one day she may have to have it again, but for now we are going to pray that day never comes and she spends her life rod-free. Even if it is for a period in life, she will be able to feel nothing in her body except what God originally put there.

Through the seasons of life, there are moments of joy and heartache. The tough part is realizing God is always with us and will see us through it all. Through those seasons, we have to remain focused on being the person God wants us to be. Grace Anna has taught me, through her struggles and miracles in life, to always dare to be the best me I can.

I challenge you to be the person you've always dreamed of being. Examine your life and decide what your priorities should be, remembering those things that bring you the most joy and matter the most to you.

Find the time to cherish the little things that truly matter. Don't get caught up in the busy rat race and forget what is truly important. Eat dinner together, write in your journal, laugh with your children, and seek opportunities to slow down life.

Be a light of hope for others even when you want to give up. Dig deep and be amazing. Reach out to those in need, not only with money but by listening, cooking their dinner, running errands for them—anything that makes their lives better.

The strength and courage I've gained through being Grace Anna's mom has catapulted me into a life I never dreamed of, a life I love with every bit of my heart. I have a wonderful family, an amazing church family, genuine friends, and peace. God has blessed beyond measure; allow Him to do the same for you.

The next time you see someone with disabilities, remember she has a God-given purpose. She is not abnormal; rather, she was created perfectly for God's plan. Treat her with respect and love, but not as if she's a pitiful burden. Every person can make a difference in our communities. Include her as an equal, not an outcast.

On those incredibly rough days, remember the spirit of a little girl who would never give up. Remember that God loves you and has a great plan for you. Remember the words Grace Anna spoke to me many days as she herself faced giants.

"It'll be okay, Momma."

ABOUT THE AUTHOR

 **Angela Ray Rodgers** was born and raised in Liberty, Kentucky. She graduated from Eastern Kentucky University with a bachelor of science in middle grades education, specializing in science and social studies, and a master of arts in instructional leadership. Angela is happily married to her husband, Jeff. They currently reside with their two wonderful children, Isaiah and Grace Anna, near Dunnville, Kentucky, where they are members of Thomas Ridge Church.

Angela taught for twelve years before beginning a new chapter in her life as an advocate for Grace Anna and other children with disabilities. She founded the Partnership for Leadership and Advocacy Network in her local community as well as becoming a leader through the Arc of Kentucky's Advocates in Action program. Angela is also involved with charities that help veterans. She and Isaiah developed the Graciebug Bundles of Love program, which creates gift baskets for children with long hospital stays and their families.

If you would like to keep up with Grace Anna,
check out Angela's blog on **graceannasings.org**,
her Facebook page at **facebook.com/angelarayrodgers**,
and her Twitter feed at **twitter.com/AngelaRayRodge1**.